GREAT YARMOUTH · LOWESTOFT

CAISTER-ON-SEA · HOPTON ON SEA

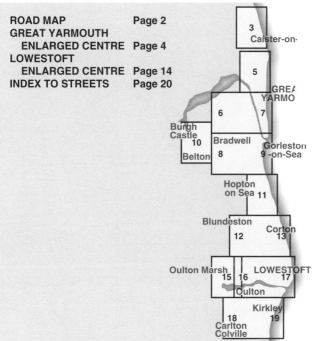

ROAD MAP Page 2
GREAT YARMOUTH ENLARGED CENTRE Page 4
LOWESTOFT ENLARGED CENTRE Page 14
INDEX TO STREETS Page 20

Every effort has been made to verify the accuracy of information in this book but the publishers cannot accept responsibility for expense or loss caused by an error or omission. Information that will be of assistance to the user of the maps will be welcomed.

The representation on these maps of a road, track or path is no evidence of the existence of a right of way.

Car Park	P
Public Convenience	C
Place of Worship	+
One-way Street	→
Pedestrianized	
Post Office	●

Scale of street plans 4 inches to 1 mile
Unless otherwise stated

Street plans prepared and published by ESTATE PUBLICATIONS, Bridewell House, TENTERDEN, KENT.
The Publishers acknowledge the co-operation of the local authorities of towns represented in this atlas.

Ordnance Survey® This product includes mapping data licensed from Ordnance Survey® with the permission of the Controller of Her Majesty's Stationery Office.

ISBN 1 84192 285 4

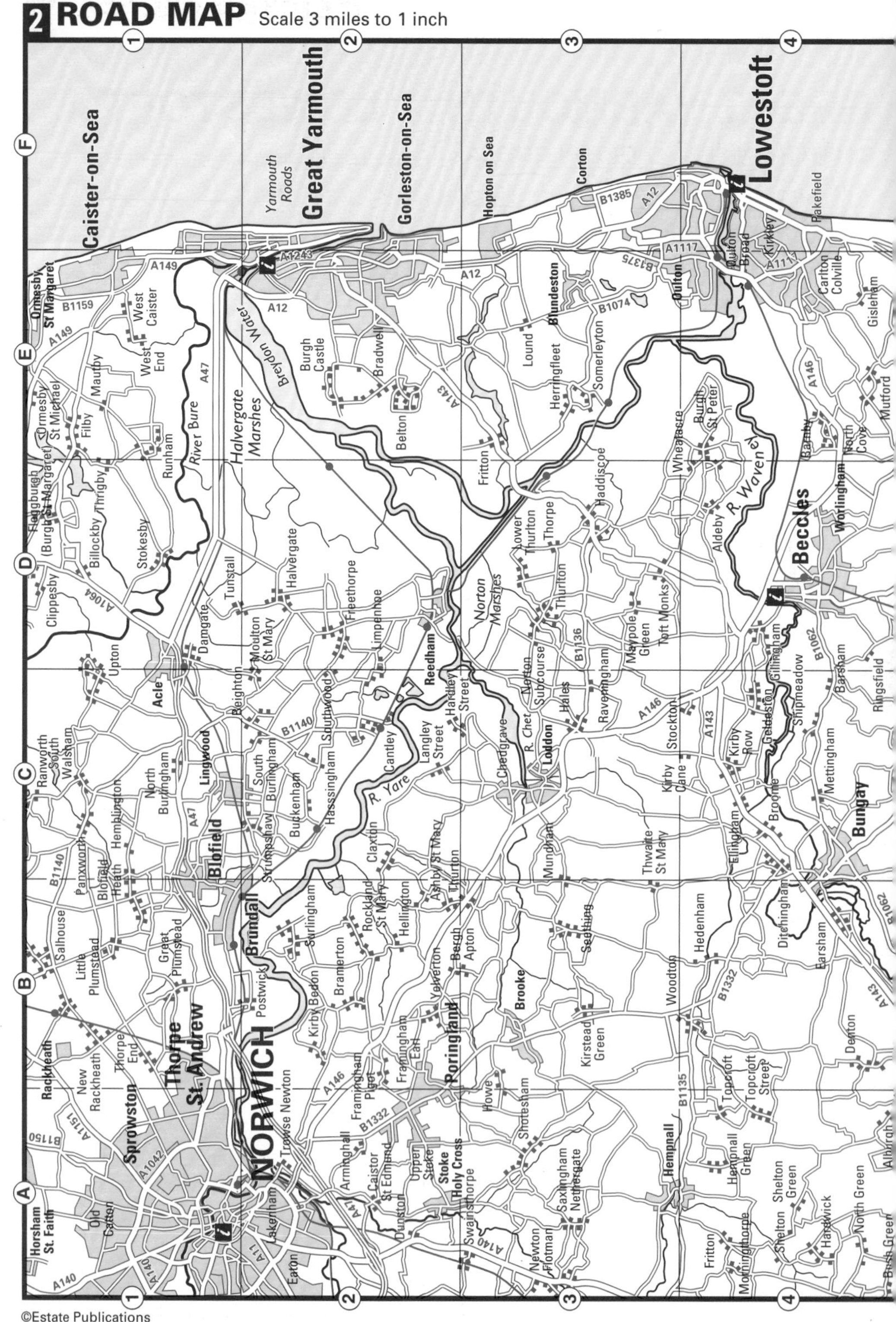

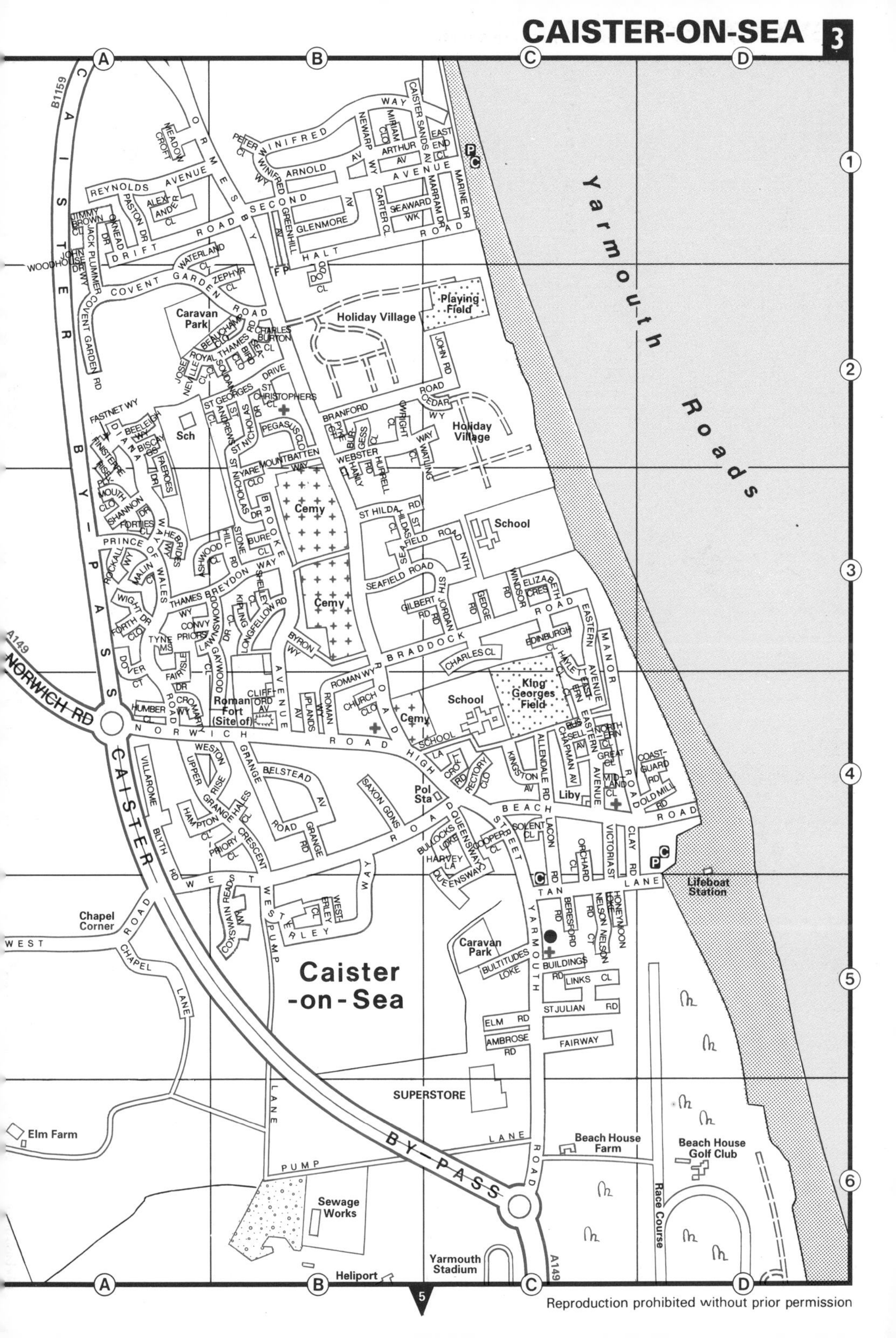

CAISTER-ON-SEA
3
A
B
C
D
1
2
3
4
5
6
Yarmouth Roads
B1159
CAISTER BY-PASS
A149
NORWICH RD
NORWICH ROAD
ORMESBY ROAD
MEADOW CROFT
REYNOLDS AVENUE
PASTON DR
ALEXANDER CL
JIMMY BROWN CL
JACK PLUMMER WAY
OKNEAD DR
JOHN WOODHOUSE DR
DRIFT ROAD
WATERLAND CL
ZEPHYR CL
COVENT GARDEN ROAD
COVENT GARDEN RD
PETER CL
WINIFRED WAY
WINIFRED WY
ARNOLD AV
SECOND AVENUE
GREENHILL AV
GLENMORE AV
FP
HALT ROAD
DOD CL
NEWARP WAY
MIRIAM CLO
ARTHUR AV
CAISTER SANDS AV
EAST END CL
CARTER CL
SEAWARD WK
MARRAM DR
MARINE DR
P
C
Caravan Park
BEAUCHAMP CLO
ROYAL THAMES CLO
BIRD CL
LEA CL
CHARLES BURTON CL
JOSE NEVILLE CL
SOUDAN CL
Holiday Village
Playing Field
JOHN RD
CEDAR WY
ST CHRISTOPHERS CL
ST GEORGES DRIVE
ST ANDREWS CL
ST NICHOLAS DR
FASTNET WY
DIANA WAY
BEELEIGH WY
BISCAY GS
FINISTERRE RISE
PLYMOUTH CLO
FAEROES DR
SHANNON DR
FORTIES CL
HEBRIDES WAY
Sch
PEGASUS CLO
MOUNTBATTEN WAY
YARE CLO
BRANFORD ROAD
PYKE CL
BURGESS CL
WRIGHT CL
WATLING WAY
WEBSTER CL
HANLY CL
HURRELL RD
Holiday Village
Cemy
BROOKE DR
BURE CL
HILL ASHWOOD
STONE RD
PRINCE OF WALES RD
ROCKALL WY
MALIN CT
WIGHT DR
FORTH CLO
DOVER CT
TYNE MS
FAIR ISLE DR
CROMARTY WY
HUMBER CL
THAMES WY
BREYDON WAY
CONVY PRIORS
LAWNSWOOD
GAYWOOD CL
KIPLING CL
SHELLEY CL
LONGFELLOW RD
BYRON WY
AVENUE
CLIFFORD AV
Roman Fort (Site of)
UPLANDS AV
ROMAN WY
ST HILDA RD
ST HILDAS CL
SEAFIELD ROAD
SEA FIELD RD NTH
School
GILBERT RD
ST JORDAN RD
SEDGE RD
WINDSOR RD
ELIZABETH CRES
EDINBURGH CL
BRADDOCK ROAD
CHARLES CL
EASTERN AVENUE
MANOR ROAD
HAYLETT CL
EAST ERN
King Georges Field
ROMAN WY
CHURCH CLO
Cemy
School
SCHOOL RD
HIGH STREET
RUSSELL AV
NORTH ERN CL
GREAT CL
MIDLAND CL
CHAPMAN AV
KINGSTON AV
ALLENDALE RD
Liby
COASTGUARD RD
OLD MILL RD
BEACH ROAD
VILLAROME
WESTON RISE
UPPER GRANGE CL
GRANGE ROAD
BELSTEAD AV
SAXON GDNS
CROFT RD
RECTORY CLO
LA
Pol Sta
HAMPTON CL
HALES CRESCENT
PRIORY CL
BLYTH RD
BULLOCKS LOKE
HARVEY LA
QUEENSWAY
COOPER CL
SOLENT CL
LACON RD
ORCHARD CL
VICTORIA ST
CLAY RD
C
P
Lifeboat Station
WEST ROAD
WESTERLEY WAY
COXSWAIN READ WAY
WEST ERLEY CL
TAN LANE
Chapel Corner
WEST ROAD
CHAPEL LANE
Caravan Park
BERESFORD RD
NELSON CT
HONEYMOON LOKE
BULTITUDES LOKE
BUILDINGS RD
LINKS CL
ST JULIAN RD
ELM RD
AMBROSE RD
FAIRWAY
YARMOUTH ROAD
Caister -on-Sea
SUPERSTORE
PUMP LANE
Elm Farm
BY-PASS
Beach House Farm
Beach House Golf Club
Race Course
Sewage Works
Yarmouth Stadium
Heliport
5

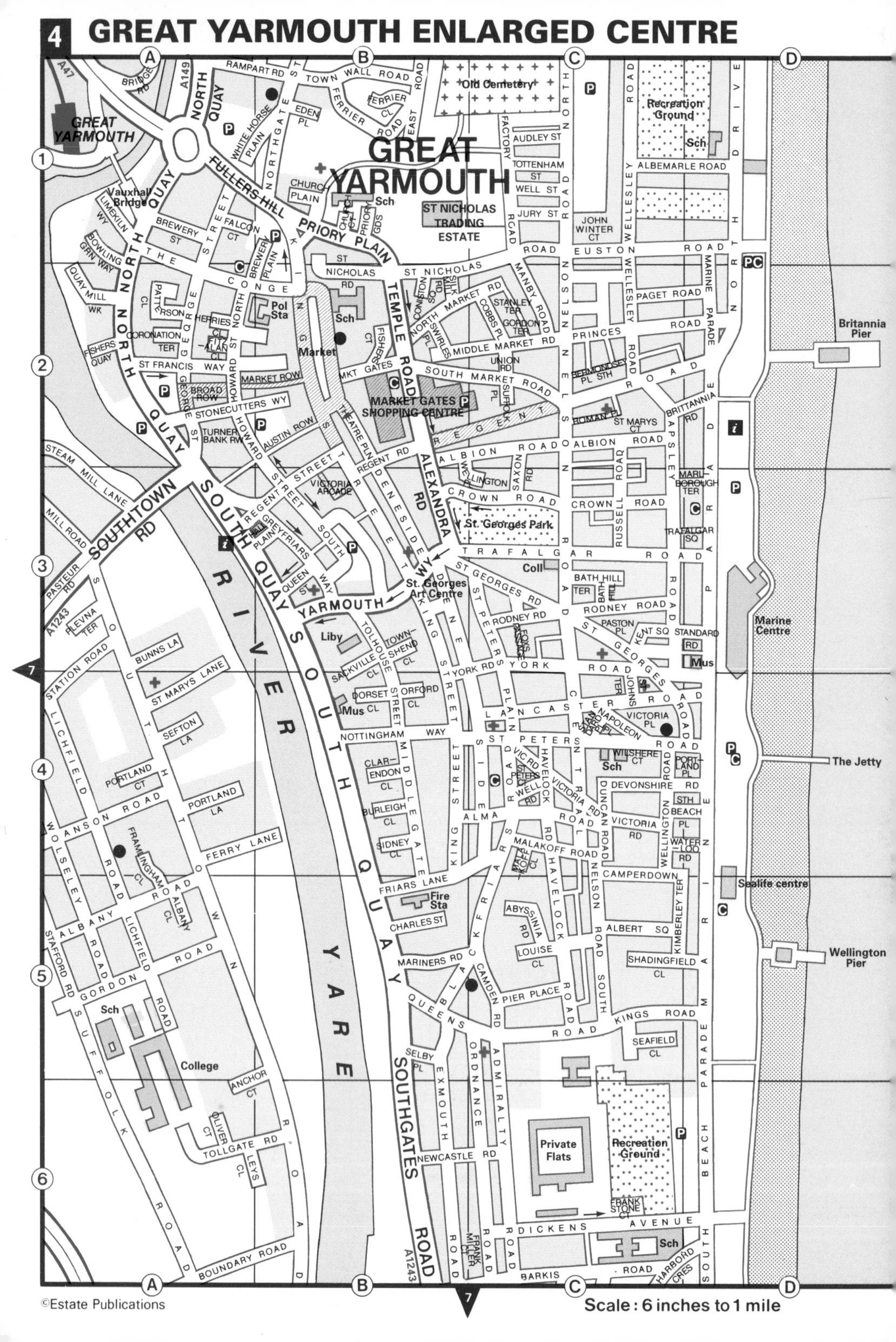

4 GREAT YARMOUTH ENLARGED CENTRE

©Estate Publications

Scale : 6 inches to 1 mile

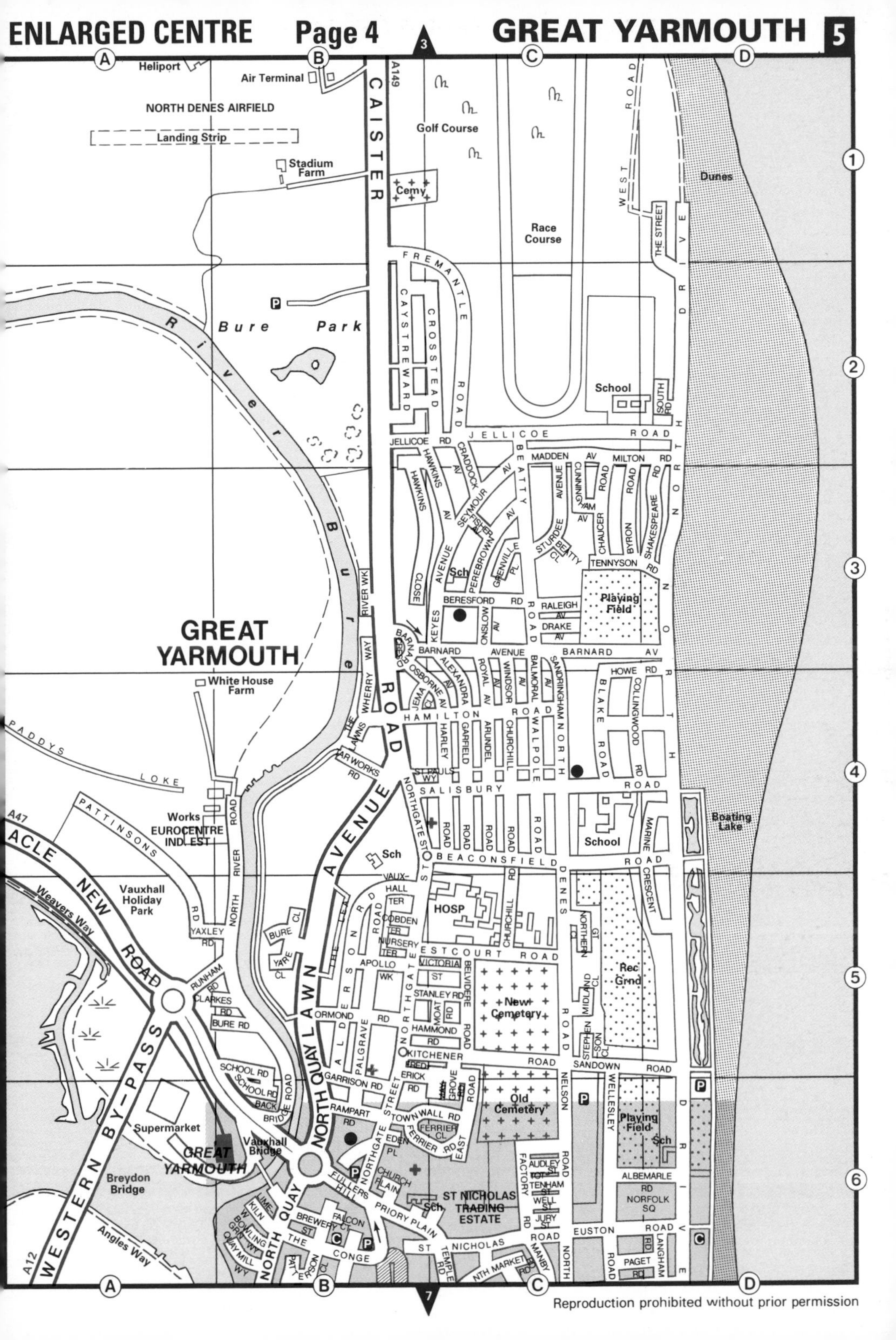
Heliport
Air Terminal
NORTH DENES AIRFIELD
Landing Strip
Stadium Farm
Golf Course
Cemy
Race Course
Dunes
WEST ROAD
THE STREET
CAISTER ROAD
A149
FREMANTLE ROAD
CAYSTREWARD
CROSSTEAD
Bure Park
River Bure
School
SOUTH RD
JELLICOE ROAD
NORTH DRIVE
MADDEN AV
MILTON RD
HAWKINS AV
HAWKINS CLOSE
CRADDOCK AV
SEYMOUR AV
FISHER AV
BEATTY ROAD
CUNNINGHAM AV
CHAUCER ROAD
BYRON ROAD
SHAKESPEARE RD
STURDEE CL
BEATTY CL
TENNYSON RD
PEREBROWN AV
GRENVILLE PL
Sch
RIVER WK
BERESFORD RD
RALEIGH AV
DRAKE AV
Playing Field
KEYES AV
ONSLOW AV
GREAT YARMOUTH
BARNARD AVENUE
BARNARD AV
WHERRY WAY
OSBORNE AV
ALEXANDRA AV
ROYAL AV
WINDSOR AV
BALMORAL AV
SANDRINGHAM AV
HOWE RD
BLAKE ROAD
COLLINGWOOD RD
White House Farm
JEMA CL
HAMILTON ROAD
THE LAWNS
HARLEY RD
GARFIELD RD
ARUNDEL RD
CHURCHILL RD
WALPOLE RD
NORTH DENES ROAD
PADDYS LOKE
AR WORKS RD
ST PAULS WY
SALISBURY ROAD
PATTINSONS
Works
EUROCENTRE IND EST
NORTH RIVER ROAD
NORTHGATE ST
Boating Lake
MARINE CRESCENT
A47
ACLE NEW ROAD
Weavers Way
Vauxhall Holiday Park
Sch
BEACONSFIELD ROAD
VAUXHALL TER
COBDEN TER
NURSERY TER
HOSP
ALDERSON ROAD
THE LEA
BURE CL
YARE CL
YAXLEY RD
NORTHERN GT CL
ESTCOURT ROAD
APOLLO WK
VICTORIA ST
STANLEY RD
MOAT RD
BELVIDERE ROAD
New Cemetery
Rec Grnd
MIDLAND CL
RUNHAM RD
CLARKES RD
BURE RD
NORTH QUAY
LAWN AVENUE
ORMOND RD
PALGRAVE
HAMMOND RD
KITCHENER RD
FRED ST
STEPHENSON CL
SCHOOL RD
SCHOOL RD BACK
BRIDGE ROAD
GARRISON RD
ERICK RD
GROVE RD
NELSON ROAD
SANDOWN ROAD
WELLESLEY
RAMPART RD
TOWN WALL RD
FERRIER CL
FERRIER RD EAST
Old Cemetery
Playing Field
Sch
Supermarket
GREAT YARMOUTH
Vauxhall Bridge
EDEN PL
NORTHGATE STREET
CHURCH PLAIN
AUDLEY ST
TOLHOUSE
TENHAM
WELL ST
JURY ST
FACTORY RD
ALBEMARLE RD
NORFOLK SQ
WESTERN BY-PASS
Breydon Bridge
FULLERS HILL
PRIORY PLAIN
ST NICHOLAS TRADING ESTATE
LIME KILN WK
BOWLING GRN WY
QUAYMILL WY
BREWERY ST
FALCON CT
THE CONGE
PATTERSON CL
ST NICHOLAS RD
TEMPLE RD
NTH MARKET RD
MANBY RD
NORTH ROAD
EUSTON ROAD
PAGET RD
LANGHAM
Angles Way
A12
A
B
C
D
1
2
3
4
5
6
3
7

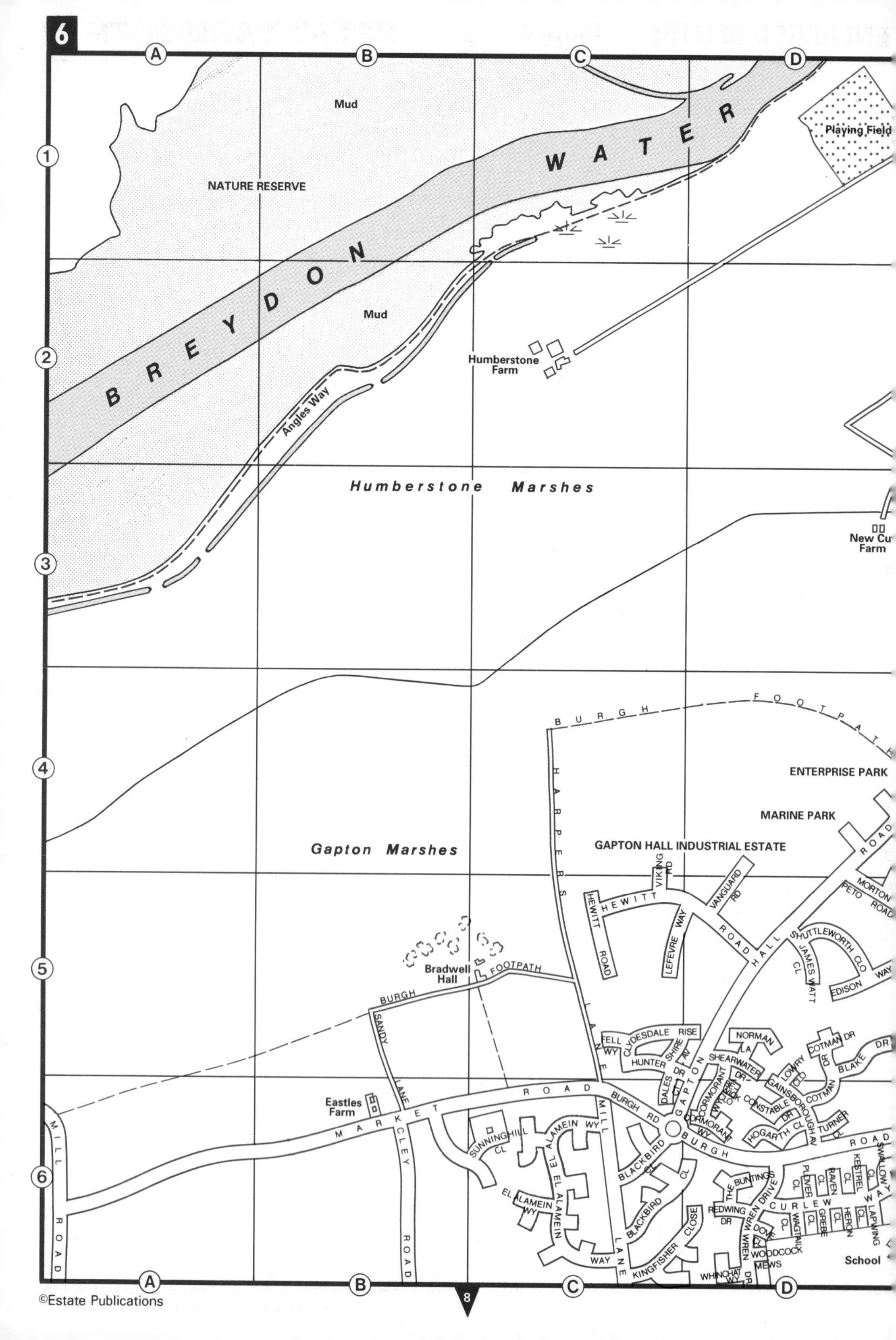
A
B
C
D
1
2
3
4
5
6
Mud
NATURE RESERVE
BREYDON WATER
Playing Field
Mud
Humberstone Farm
Angles Way
Humberstone Marshes
New Cu
Farm
BURGH FOOTPATH
ENTERPRISE PARK
MARINE PARK
GAPTON HALL INDUSTRIAL ESTATE
Gapton Marshes
HARPERS LANE
HEWITT ROAD
VIKING RD
VANGUARD RD
LEFEVRE WAY
GAPTON HALL ROAD
MORTON
PETO ROAD
SHUTTLEWORTH CLO
JAMES WATT CL
EDISON WAY
Bradwell Hall
FOOTPATH
BURGH
SANDY LANE
FELL WY
CLYDESDALE RISE
SHIRE AV
HUNTER DR
DALES CT
NORMAN LA
SHEARWATER DR
CORMORANT WY
CONSTABLE DR
GAINSBOROUGH AV
LOWRY CL
COTMAN DR
BLAKE DR
TURNER CL
HOGARTH CL
Eastles Farm
MARKET ROAD
BURGH RD
MILL LANE
SUNNINGHILL CL
EL ALAMEIN WY
EL ALAMEIN WAY
BLACKBIRD CL
CLEY ROAD
BURGH ROAD
THE BUNTINGS
REDWING DR
WREN DRIVE
CURLEW WAY
PLOVER CL
RAVEN CL
KESTREL CL
SWALLOW
WAGTAIL CL
GREBE CL
HERON CL
LAPWING
DOVE CL
WOODCOCK MEWS
KINGFISHER CLOSE
WHINCHAT WY
WREN DR
School
MILL ROAD

8

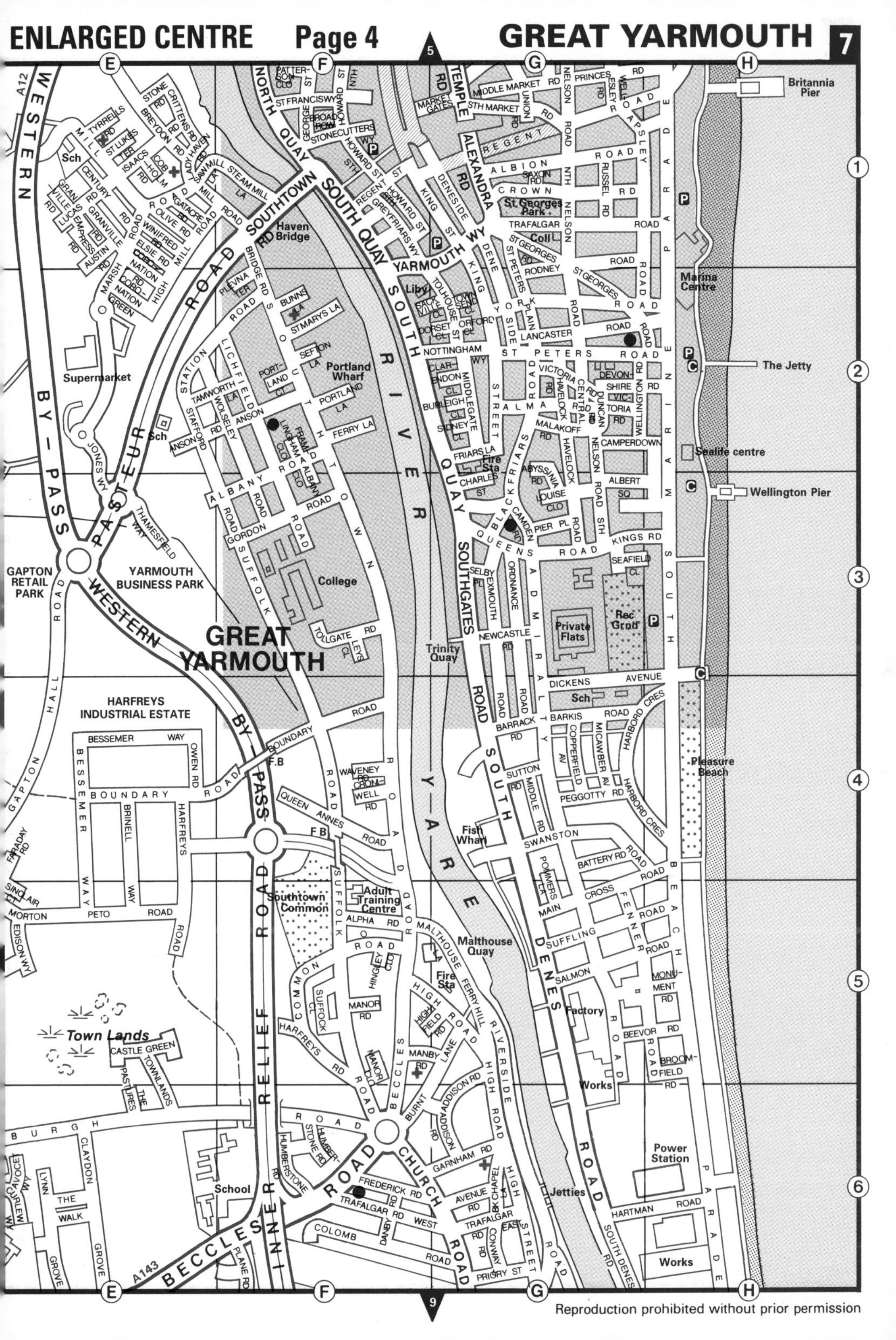
GREAT YARMOUTH
Britannia Pier
The Jetty
Wellington Pier
Sealife centre
Marina Centre
Pleasure Beach
Power Station
Haven Bridge
Portland Wharf
College
Trinity Quay
Fish Wharf
Malthouse Quay
Jetties
Southtown Common
Adult Training Centre
Town Lands
GAPTON RETAIL PARK
YARMOUTH BUSINESS PARK
HARFREYS INDUSTRIAL ESTATE
Supermarket
Private Flats
Rec Grnd
St Georges Park
RIVER YARE
SOUTH QUAY
SOUTHTOWN ROAD
WESTERN BY-PASS
INNER RELIEF ROAD
BECCLES ROAD
SOUTH DENES ROAD
MARINE PARADE
SOUTH BEACH PARADE

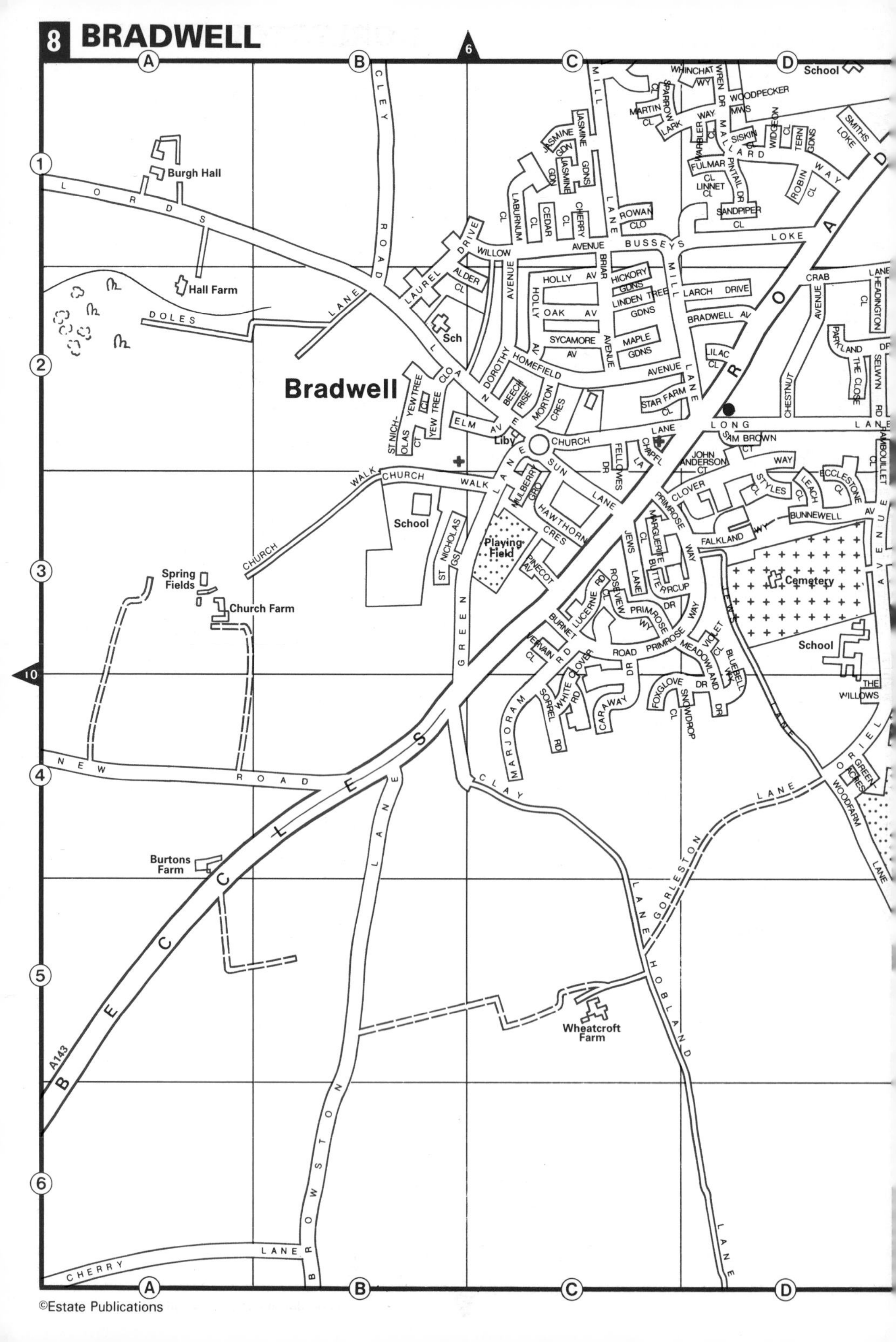

8 BRADWELL

Bradwell

Burgh Hall
Hall Farm
DOLES
LORDS
CLEY ROAD
LANE

Spring Fields
Church Farm
School
CHURCH WALK
ST NICHOLAS GS

NEW ROAD
Burtons Farm

BEECCLES LANE
A143
B

CHERRY LANE
BROWSTON LANE

LAUREL DRIVE
ALDER CL
WILLOW
Sch
St NICHOLAS CT
YEWTREE
YEW TREE
ELM AV
Liby
CHURCH WALK
MULBERRY
SUN LANE
HAWTHORN CRES
PINECOT AV
GREEN
LAURINUM
CEDAR
CHERRY
AVENUE
HOLLY AV
HOLLY
OAK AV
SYCAMORE AV
HOMEFIELD
DOROTHY
BEECH RISE
MORTON CRES
CHURCH
BRIAR
HICKORY GDNS
LINDEN TREE GDNS
MAPLE GDNS
STAR FARM
CHAPEL LANE
FELLOWES
MARGUERITE
JEWS
PRIMROSE WAY
BITTE
BURCUP
ROSSVIEW RD
LICERNE RD
GERMAN CT
BURNET CT
WHITE CLOVER RD
SORREL RD
MARJORAM
CLAY LANE
CARAWAY
SORREL RD
PRIMROSE ROAD
FOXGLOVE
SNOWDROP
VIOLET
MEADOWLAND
BLUEBELL

Playing Field
School

JASMINE GDN
JASMINE GDNS
BUSSEYS
ROWAN CLO
LARCH DRIVE
BRADWELL AV
LILAC CL
AVENUE
LANE
MILL LANE
ROAD LOKE
LONG
SAM BROWN
JOHN ANDERSON CT
CLOVER WAY
FALKLAND WY
STYLES
LEACH
BUNNEWELL AV
ECCLESTONE
Cemetery
School
THE WILLOWS

WHINCHAT WY
WREN WY
SPARROW
MARTIN
LARK
WARBLER WAY
SISKIN
FULMAR CL
LINNET CL
SANDPIPER CL
ROBIN CL
PINTAIL DR
WOODPECKER MWS
WIDGEON
TERN GDNS
SMITHS LORE
WAY
School

CRAB AVENUE
CHESTNUT LANE
HEADINGTON RD
PARKLAND DR
THE CLOSE
SELWYN RD
RAMBOULET
AMBOULET
SELWYN AVENUE
GREEN
WOODFARM
THE WILLOWS
GORLESTON LANE
HOBLAND LANE
Wheatcroft Farm

©Estate Publications

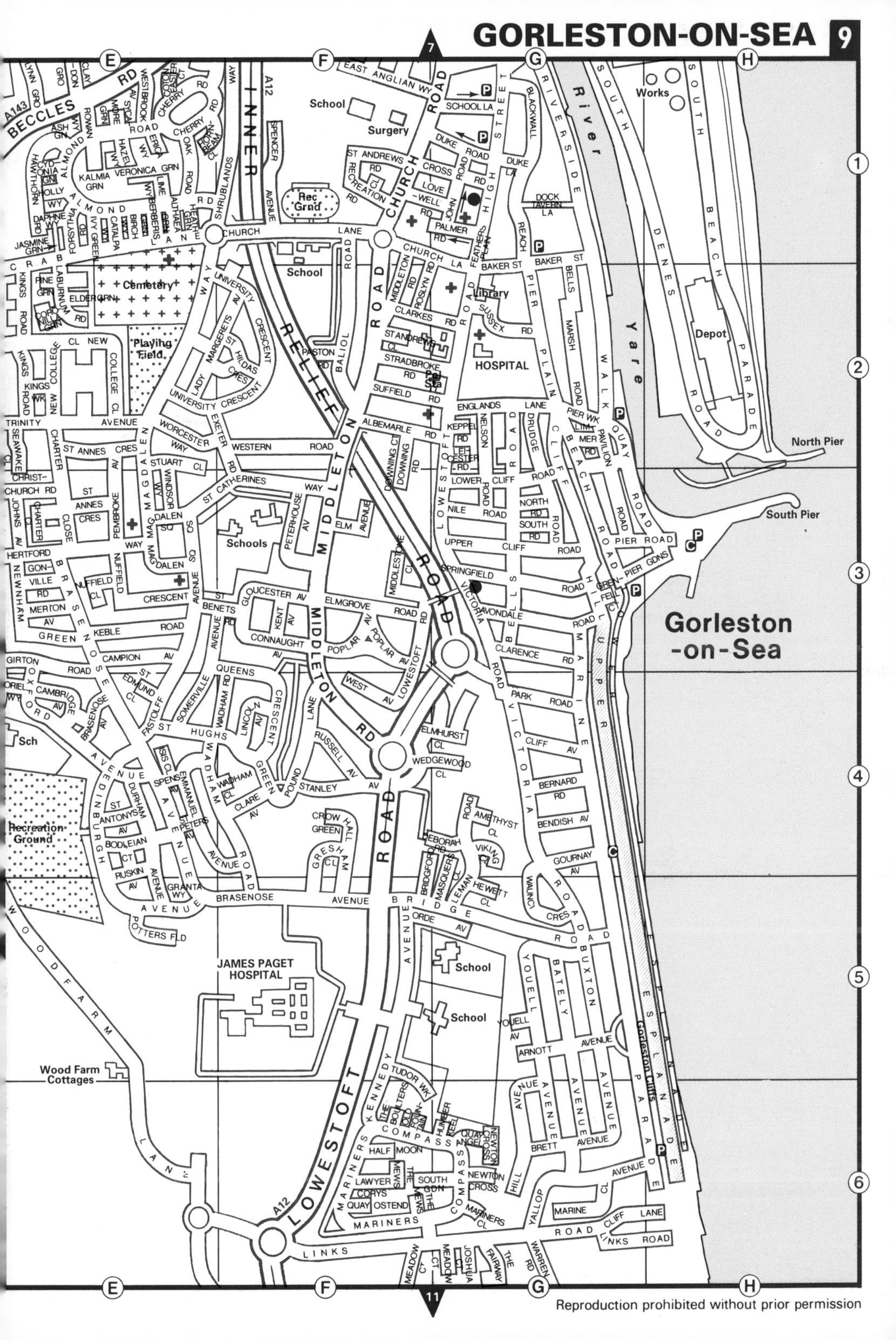
Gorleston
-on-Sea
River Yare
North Pier
South Pier
Works
Depot
School
Surgery
Rec Grnd
Cemetery
Playing Field
Library
HOSPITAL
Pol Sta
Schools
Sch
Recreation Ground
JAMES PAGET HOSPITAL
Wood Farm Cottages
Gorleston Cliffs
BECCLES RD
A143
A12
INNER RELIEF ROAD
CHURCH LANE
CHURCH ROAD
HIGH STREET
BAKER ST
PIER PLAIN
RIVERSIDE
SOUTH DENES
SOUTH BEACH PARADE
QUAY ROAD
PIER ROAD
PIER GDNS
UPPER CLIFF ROAD
LOWER CLIFF ROAD
MARINE PARADE
UPPER PROMENADE
LOWER ESPLANADE
MIDDLETON ROAD
LOWESTOFT ROAD
VICTORIA ROAD
CRAB LANE
UNIVERSITY CRESCENT
MAGDALEN WAY
BRASENOSE AVENUE
WOODFARM LANE
LINKS ROAD
BRIDGE ROAD
BUXTON AVENUE
YALLOP AVENUE
EAST ANGLIAN WY
ELMGROVE ROAD
STANLEY AV
CLIFF LANE
LINKS ROAD
WARREN RD

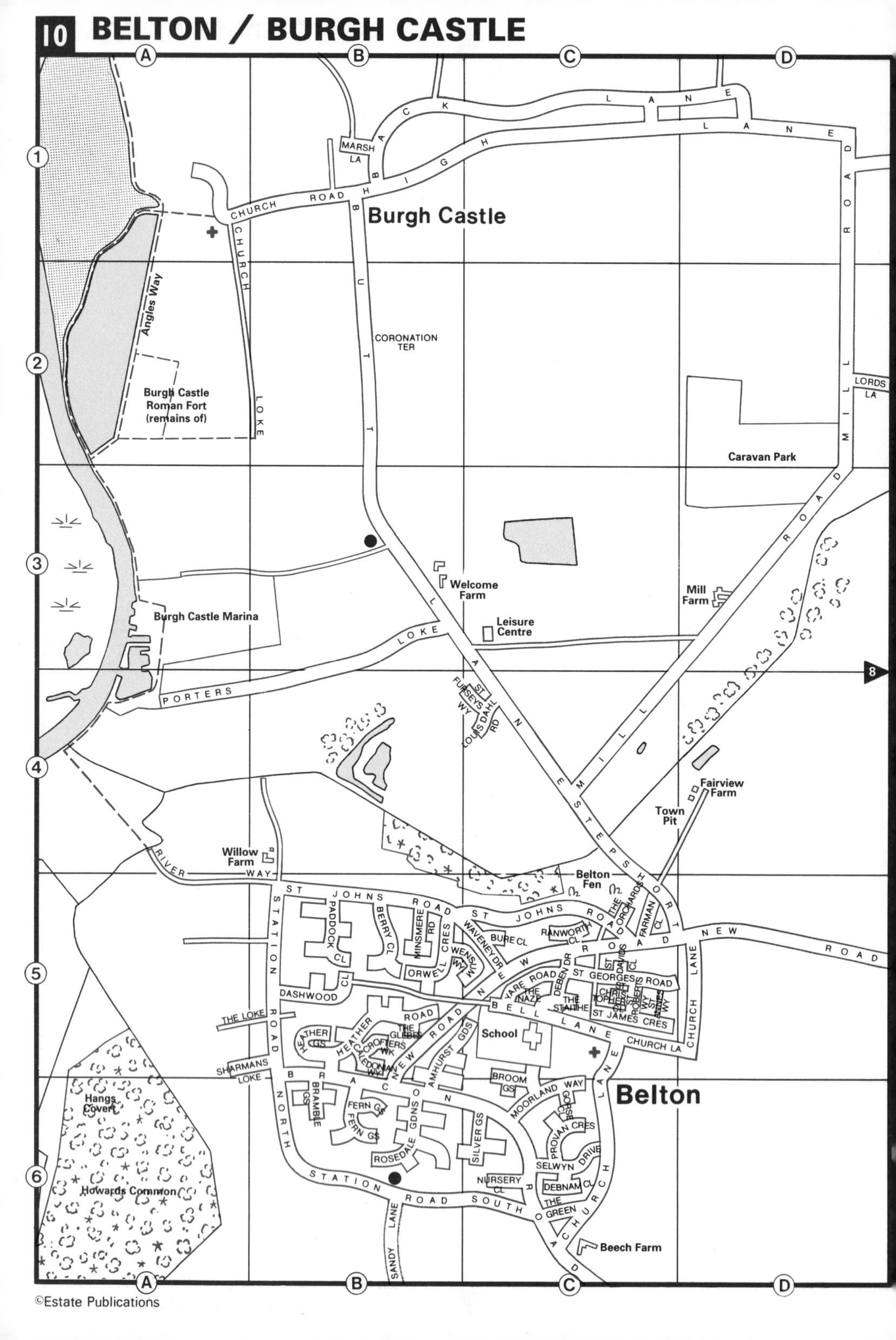

10 BELTON / BURGH CASTLE

Burgh Castle

Burgh Castle Roman Fort (remains of)

Angles Way

MARSH LA

BACK LANE

BIGH ROAD

CHURCH ROAD

CHURCH LOKE

CORONATION TER

BUCT

LOKE

Welcome Farm

Leisure Centre

Caravan Park

Mill Farm

Burgh Castle Marina

PORTERS

LOKE

LANE

FULSYSHALL WY

ST LOUIS DAHL RD

STEPSHORT

MILL ROAD

LORDS LA

Fairview Farm

Town Pit

RIVER

WAY

Willow Farm

Belton Fen

ST JOHNS ROAD

STATION ROAD

PADDOCK CL

BERRY CL

MINSMERE

WAVENEY DR

BURE CL

RANWORTH CL

ORCHARD CL

YARMAN CL

NEW ROAD

CHURCH LANE

DASHWOOD

ORWELL CL

WENSUM

VARE ROAD

THE STAITHE

ST GEORGE'S ROAD

ST JAMES CRES

CHURCH LA

THE LOKE

HEATHER GS

HEATHER

THE GLEBE

CROFTERS WK

BELL LANE

School

Belton

SHARMANS LOKE

BRAMBLE

FERN GS

FERN GS

AMHURST GDNS

SILVER GS

BROOM

MOORLAND WAY

PROVAN CRES

SELWYN DRIVE

CHURCH

Hangs Covert

NORTH STATION ROAD

ROSEDALE GDNS

NURSERY CL

THE GREEN

DEBNAM

Howards Common

SANDY LANE

STATION ROAD SOUTH

Beech Farm

8

©Estate Publications

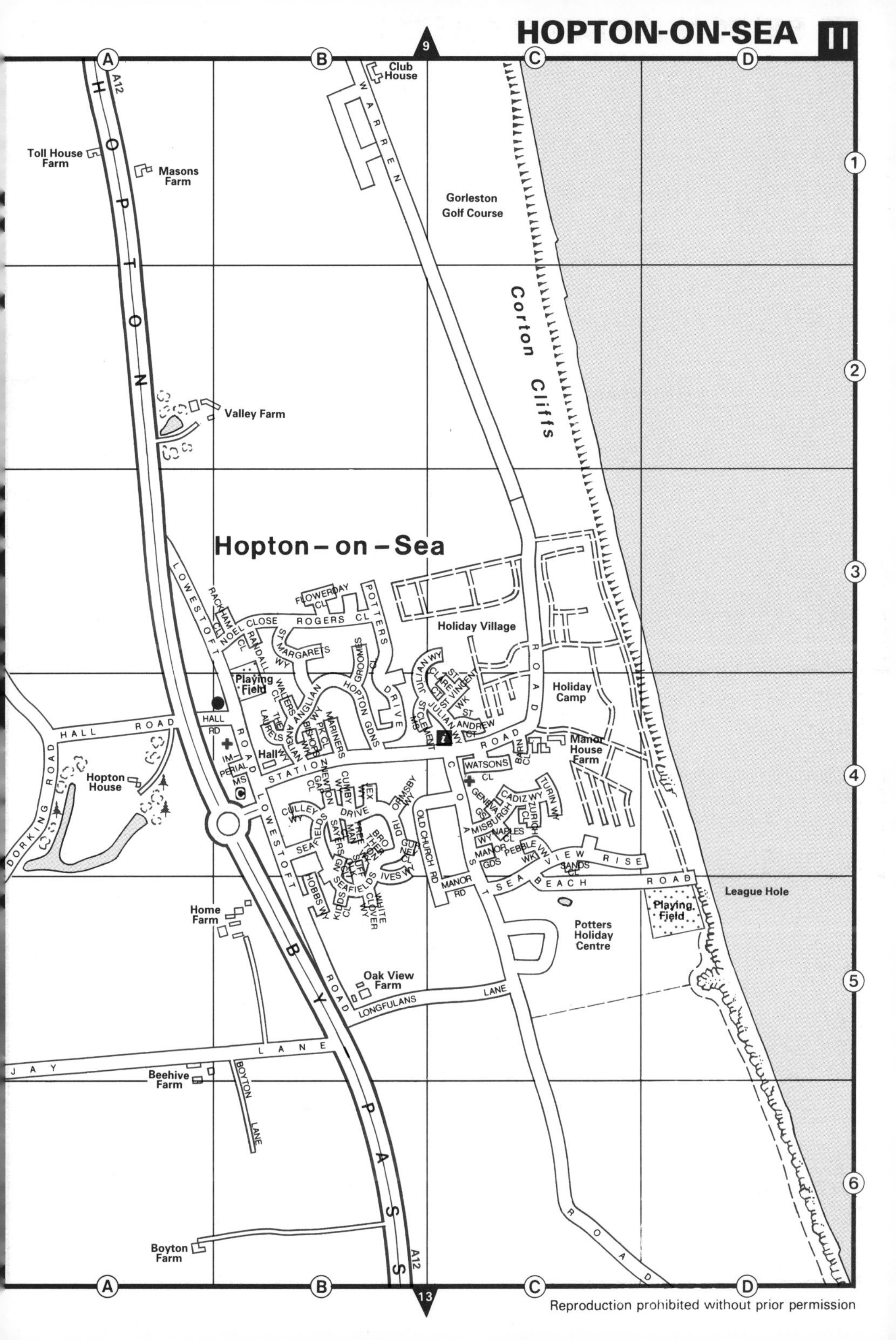
Hopton-on-Sea
Club House
Gorleston Golf Course
Corton Cliffs
Toll House Farm
Masons Farm
Valley Farm
Holiday Village
Holiday Camp
Manor House Farm
Playing Field
Hall
Hopton House
League Hole
Potters Holiday Centre
Home Farm
Oak View Farm
Beehive Farm
Boyton Farm
HOPTON ROAD
HOPTON BY PASS
A12
WARREN ROAD
LOWESTOFT ROAD
HALL ROAD
DORKING ROAD
STATION ROAD
COAST ROAD
BEACH ROAD
LONGFULANS LANE
JAY LANE
BOYTON LANE
VIEW RISE
OLD CHURCH RD
MANOR RD
MANOR GDS
WATSONS CL
ROGERS CL
POTTERS DRIVE
NOEL CLOSE
FLOWERDAY CL
ST MARGARETS WY
HOPTON GDNS
ANGLIAN WY
MARINERS
SEAFIELDS
CULLEY WY
CUMBY WY
IVES WY
WHITE CLOVER WY
HOBBS WY
KIDDS CL
CADIZ WY
TURIN WY
ZURICH CL
NAPLES CL
PEBBLE VW
SANDS CL
GENEVA GS
MISBURGH
JULIAN WY
ST VINCENT WK
ST ANDREW CT
ST CLEMENT MS
ORMSBY WY
A B C D
1 2 3 4 5 6
9
13

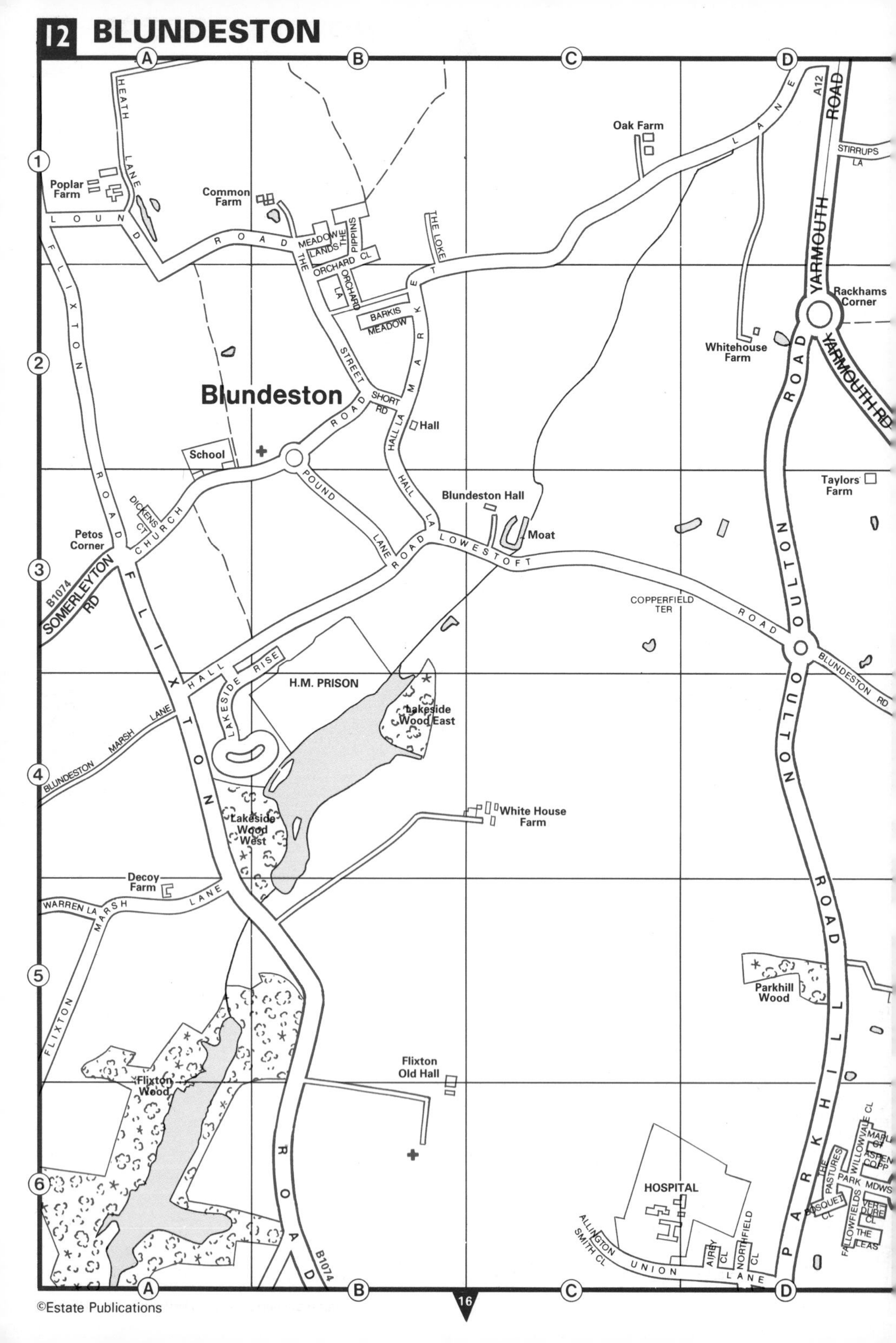
12
BLUNDESTON
A
B
C
D
1
2
3
4
5
6
Blundeston
HEATH LANE
LOUND ROAD
Poplar Farm
Common Farm
MEADOW LANDS
THE PIPPINS
ORCHARD CL
THE ORCHARD
ORCHARD LA
THE LOKE
BARKIS MEADOW
MARKET LANE
Oak Farm
A12
YARMOUTH ROAD
STIRRUPS LA
Rackhams Corner
YARMOUTH RD
Whitehouse Farm
FLIXTON ROAD
THE STREET
SHORT RD
ROAD
HALL LA
Hall
School
POUND LANE
DICKENS CT
CHURCH
Petos Corner
B1074
SOMERLEYTON RD
Blundeston Hall
Moat
LOWESTOFT ROAD
Taylors Farm
COPPERFIELD TER
OULTON ROAD
BLUNDESTON RD
HALL
LAKESIDE RISE
H.M. PRISON
Lakeside Wood East
BLUNDESTON MARSH LANE
Lakeside Wood West
White House Farm
Decoy Farm
WARREN LA
MARSH LANE
FLIXTON
Flixton Wood
Flixton Old Hall
Parkhill Wood
PARK HILL
HOSPITAL
ALLINGTON SMITH CL
UNION LANE
AIRBY CL
NORTHFIELD CL
WILLOWVALE CL
THE PASTURES
PARK MDWS
BOSQUET CL
FALLOWFIELDS
THE LEAS
16
©Estate Publications

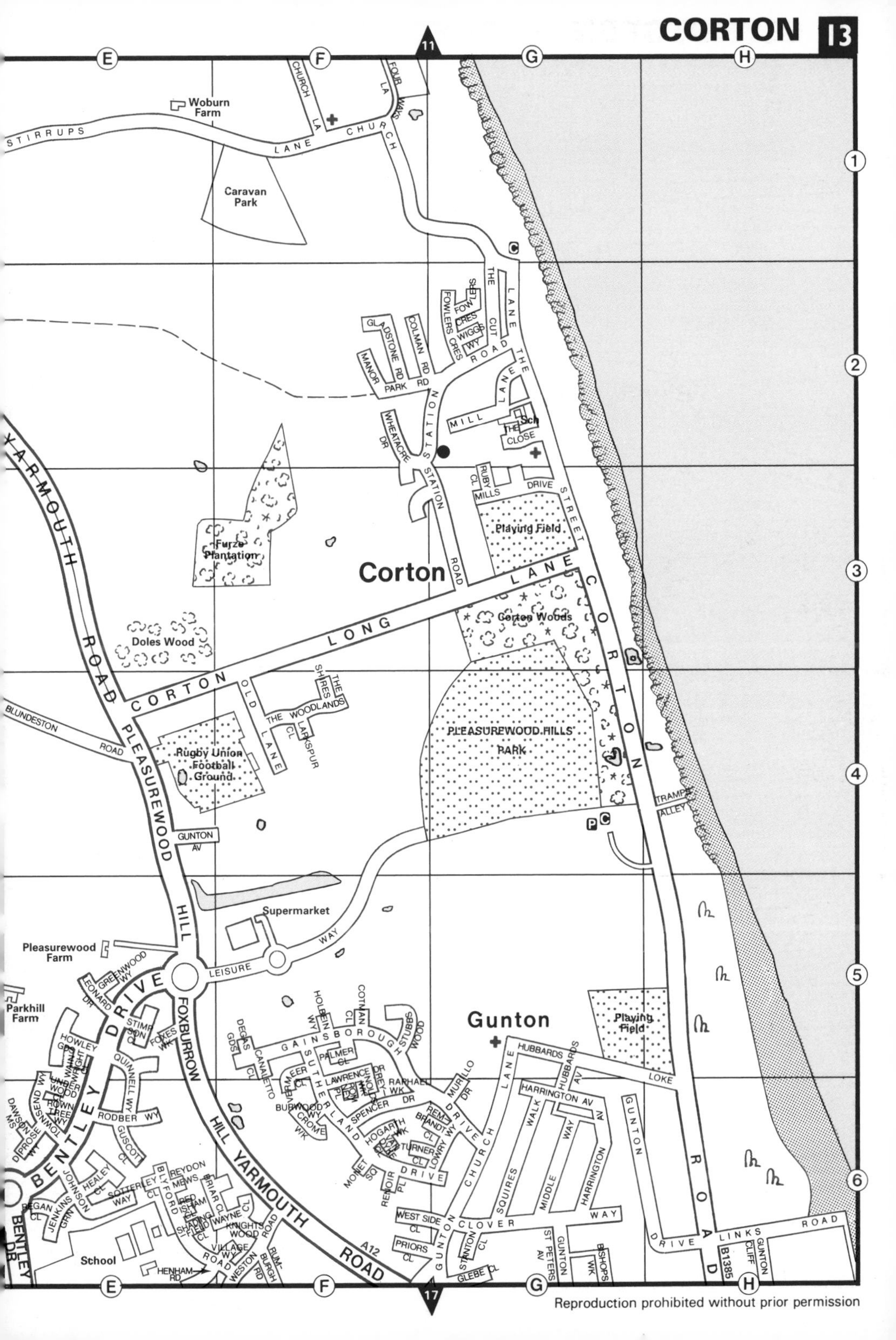

Woburn Farm
STIRRUPS LANE
CHURCH LA
CHURCH LANE
FOUR WAYS
Caravan Park
THE CUT
LANE
FOWLERS CRES
WIGGS WY
GLADSTONE RD
COLMAN RD
MANOR PARK RD
ROAD
THE LANE
MILL LANE
THE CLOSE
Sch
WHEATACRE DR
STATION ROAD
RUBY CL
MILLS DRIVE
STREET
Playing Field
Furze Plantation
Corton
LONG LANE
Corton Woods
CORTON
YARMOUTH ROAD
Doles Wood
THE SHIRES
THE WOODLANDS
OLD LANE
LARKSPUR CL
BLUNDESTON ROAD
PLEASUREWOOD
Rugby Union Football Ground
PLEASUREWOOD HILLS PARK
TRAMPS ALLEY
GUNTON AV
HILL
Supermarket
LEISURE WAY
Pleasurewood Farm
GREENWOOD WY
LEONARD DR
Parkhill Farm
STIMPSON CL
FOXES WK
FOXBURROW
HOWLEY GDS
DRIVE
QUINNELL WY
HOLBEIN WY
COTMAN CL
STUBBS WOOD
DEGAS GDS
CANALETTO CL
GAINSBOROUGH
PALMER CL
SUTHERLAND
LAWRENCE
CONSTABLE
RAPHAEL WK
MURILLO DR
VERMEER CL
BURWOOD WY
CROME WK
SPENCER DR
REMBRANDT WY
HOGARTH WK
TURNER CL
LOWRY WY
MONET SQ
RENOIR PL
DRIVE
Gunton
HUBBARDS LOKE
HUBBARDS AV
HARRINGTON AV
WALK
WAY
GUNTON DRIVE
ROAD
Playing Field
TOWNSEND WY
DAWSON MS
PROSE WY
BENTLEY DR
RODBER WY
GUSCOTT CL
HEALEY CL
JOHNSON GRN
JENKINS
REGAN CL
SOTTERLEY WAY
BLYFORD CL
REYDON MEWS
BRIAR CL
WAYNE CL
KNIGHTS WOOD
SHADING FIELD
VILLAGE WY
HILL YARMOUTH ROAD
A12
School
HENHAM RD
WESTON RD
RUMBURGH RD
WEST SIDE CL
PRIORS CL
GUNTON CLOVER
CHURCH LANE
SQUIRES
MIDDLE
HARRINGTON WAY
STANTON CL
GLEBE CL
ST PETERS AV
GUNTON AV
BISHOPS WK
LINKS ROAD
B1385
GUNTON CLIFF
E F G H
1 2 3 4 5 6
11
17

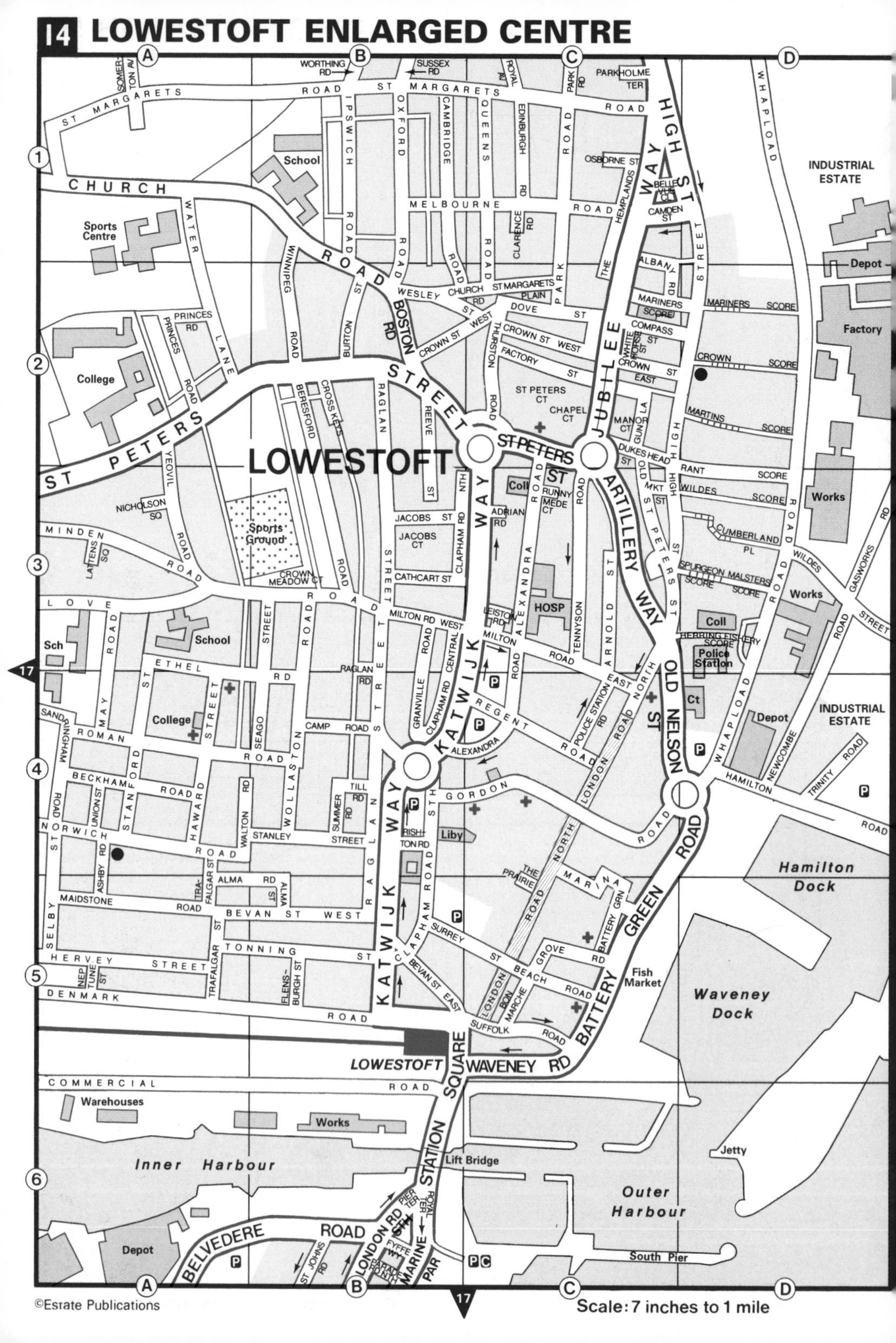

14 LOWESTOFT ENLARGED CENTRE

©Estate Publications

Scale: 7 inches to 1 mile

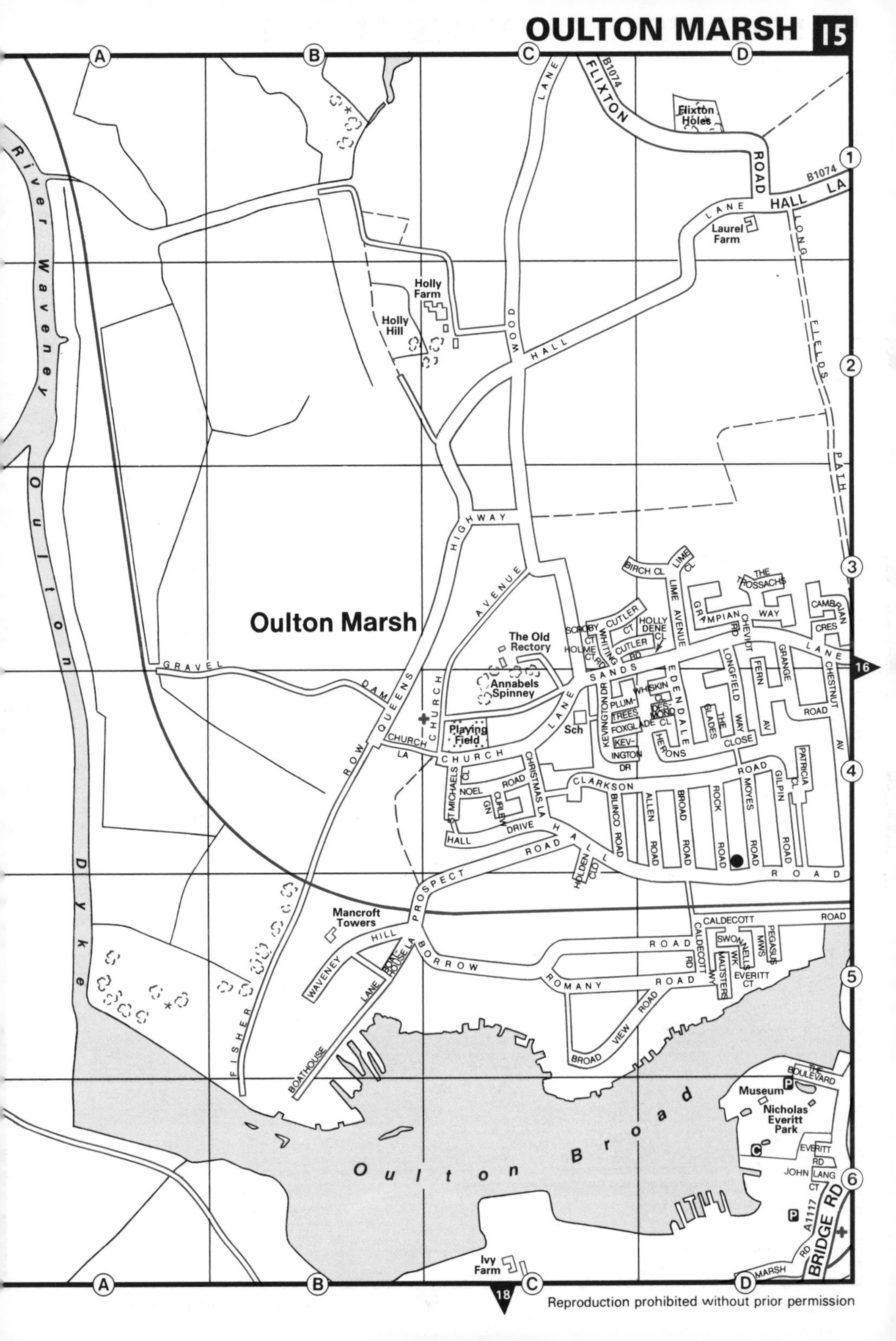
Oulton Marsh
River Waveney
Oulton Dyke
Oulton Broad
Flixton Holes
FLIXTON ROAD
B1074
HALL LA
LANE
Laurel Farm
LONG FIELDS PATH
Holly Farm
Holly Hill
WOOD LANE
HALL
HIGHWAY
AVENUE
QUEENS ROW
GRAVEL DAM
CHURCH LA
CHURCH
The Old Rectory
Annabels Spinney
Playing Field
Sch
SANDS LANE
BIRCH CL
LIME CL
LIME AVENUE
CUTLER CT
CUTLER RD
HOLLY DENE CL
SCROBY CT
WHITING RD
HOLME CT
THE TROSSACHS
GRAMPIAN RD
WAY
CAMBRIAN CRES
CHEVIOT
LANE
GRANGE ROAD
CHESTNUT AV
FERN AV
LONGFIELD WAY
CLOSE
THE GLADES
EDENDALE
HERONS
WHISKIN CL
DESMOND CL
PLUMTREES
FOXGLADE
KEVINGTON DR
KEVINGTON DR
CLARKSON ROAD
ST MICHAELS CL
NOEL
ROAD
CURLEW GN
CHRISTMAS LA
HALL DRIVE
HALL ROAD
BLINCO ROAD
ALLEN ROAD
BROAD ROAD
ROCK ROAD
MOYES ROAD
GILPIN ROAD
PATRICIA CL
ROAD
HOLDEN CLO
PROSPECT ROAD
Mancroft Towers
WAVENEY HILL
BOATHOUSE LA
BORROW ROAD
LANE
BOATHOUSE
CALDECOTT ROAD
CALDECOTT RD
SWONNELLS WK
MALTSTERS WY
MWS
PEGASUS
EVERITT CT
ROMANY ROAD
BROAD VIEW ROAD
FISHER
THE BOULEVARD
Museum
Nicholas Everitt Park
EVERITT RD
JOHN LANG CT
A1117
BRIDGE RD
MARSH RD
Ivy Farm
A B C D
1 2 3 4 5 6
16
18

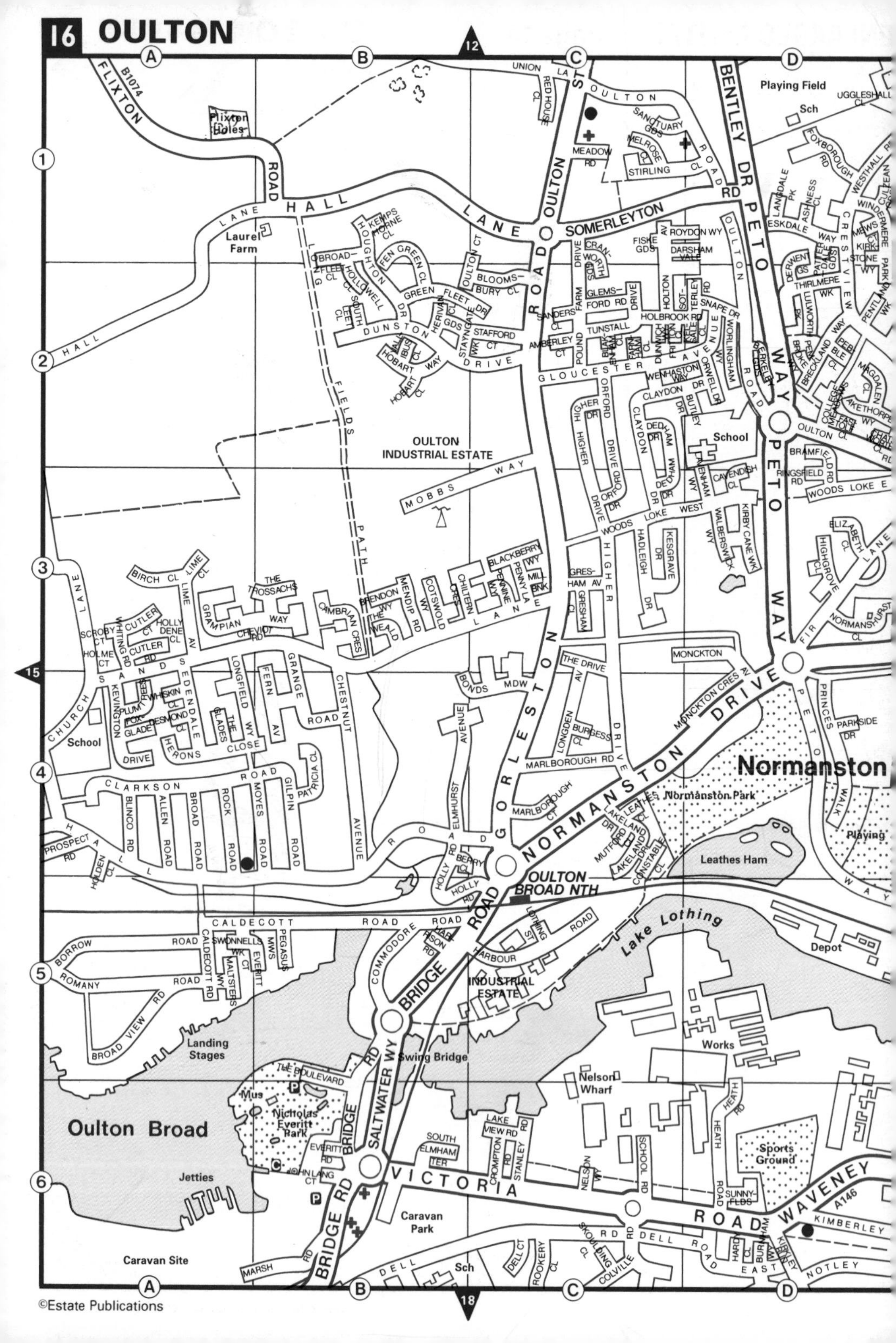

16
OULTON
A
B
C
D
12
15
18
1
2
3
4
5
6
FLIXTON ROAD
B1074
Flixton Holes
HALL LANE
Laurel Farm
UNION LA
RED HOUSE CL
OULTON ST
SANCTUARY GDS
MELROSE CL
MEADOW RD
STIRLING CL
BENTLEY DR
PETO WAY
Playing Field
Sch
UGGLESHALL CL
FOXBOROUGH
WESTHALL RD
LANGDALE PK
ASHNESS CL
ESKDALE WAY
CRESTVIEW
WINDERMERE PARK
DERWENT GS
THIRLMERE WK
LULWORTH PK
PENTLAND
BRECKLAND WAY
MAGDALEN
LAKETHORPE
OULTON ROAD
SOMERLEYTON
ROYDON WY
FISKE GDS
DARSHAM VALE
GLEMSFORD RD
HOLBROOK RD
SNAPE DR
TUNSTALL
AMBERLEY CT
POUND FARM DRIVE
SANDERS CL
GLOUCESTER AVENUE
WENHASTON WAY
WORLINGHAM
CLAYDON DR
BUTLEY DR
ORWELL DR
HIGHER DR
ORFORD DRIVE
DEDHAM DR
School
BRAMFIELD RD
RINGSFIELD RD
CAVENDISH CL
WOODS LOKE EAST
WOODS LOKE WEST
KIRBY CANE WK
WALBERSWICK WY
HADLEIGH DR
KESGRAVE DR
ELIZABETH CL
HIGHGROVE CL
FIR LANE
NORMANSHURST CL
KEMPS HORNE CL
BROADFLEET CL
HOUGHTON
HOLLOWELL CL
SOUTH LEET CL
FEN GREEN CL
GREEN FLEET DR
OULTON CT
BLOOMSBURY CL
DUNSTON DRIVE
HERIVAN GDS
STAYNGATE WK
STAFFORD CT
HOBART WAY
HOBART CL
FIELDS PATH
LONG
OULTON INDUSTRIAL ESTATE
MOBBS WAY
BLACKBERRY WY
PENNY LA
MILL BNK
PENNINE
CHILTERN
COTSWOLD WY
MENDIP RD
BRENDON WY
THE WEALD
CAMBRIAN CRES
THE TROSSACHS
GRAMPIAN WAY
CHEVIOT RD
BIRCH CL
LIME CL
LIME AV
CUTLER CT
CUTLER RD
HOLLY DENE CL
SCROBY CT
WHITING RD
HOLME CT
SANDS LANE
CHURCH LANE
School
KEVINGTON
PLUM
FOXGLADE
WHISKIN
DESMOND CL
EDENDALE
HERONS
GLADES
LONGFIELD WY
FERN AV
GRANGE ROAD
CHESTNUT AVENUE
CLOSE
CLARKSON ROAD
BLINCO RD
ALLEN ROAD
BROAD ROAD
ROCK ROAD
MOVES ROAD
GILPIN ROAD
PATRICIA CL
GRESHAM AV
GRESHAM CL
HIGHER DRIVE
MONCKTON
MONCKTON CRES AV
THE DRIVE AV
BONDS MDW
AVENUE
ELMHURST
LONGDEN AV
BURGESS CL
MARLBOROUGH RD
GORLESTON ROAD
NORMANSTON DRIVE
Normanston
Normanston Park
PRINCES WALK
PARKSIDE DR
Playing
LEATHES
LAKELAND DR
MUTFORD
CONSTABLE CL
Leathes Ham
PROSPECT RD
HOLDEN CL
HALL ROAD
HOLLY RD
BERRY CL
OULTON BROAD NTH
CALDECOTT ROAD
BORROW ROAD
ROMANY ROAD
SWONNELLS WK
CALDECOTT RD
PEGASUS MWS
EVERITT CT
MALTSTERS WY
COMMODORE ROAD
HARRISON RD
LOTHING ST
HARBOUR ROAD
Lake Lothing
Depot
INDUSTRIAL ESTATE
BRIDGE ROAD
BROAD VIEW RD
Landing Stages
Works
Swing Bridge
SALTWATER WY
THE BOULEVARD
Mus
Nicholas Everitt Park
EVERITT RD
JOHN LANG CT
Oulton Broad
Jetties
Nelson Wharf
LAKE VIEW RD
SOUTH ELMHAM TER
CROMPTON RD
STANLEY RD
NELSON WY
SCHOOL RD
HEATH RD
HEATH ROAD
Sports Ground
SUNNY FLDS
VICTORIA ROAD
WAVENEY
A146
KIMBERLEY
Caravan Park
Caravan Site
MARSH RD
BRIDGE RD
DELL RD
DELL ROAD EAST
Sch
DELL CT
ROOKERY CL
SKOULDING CL
COLVILLE
HARDY CL
BURNHAM
KIRKLEY
NOTLEY
©Estate Publications

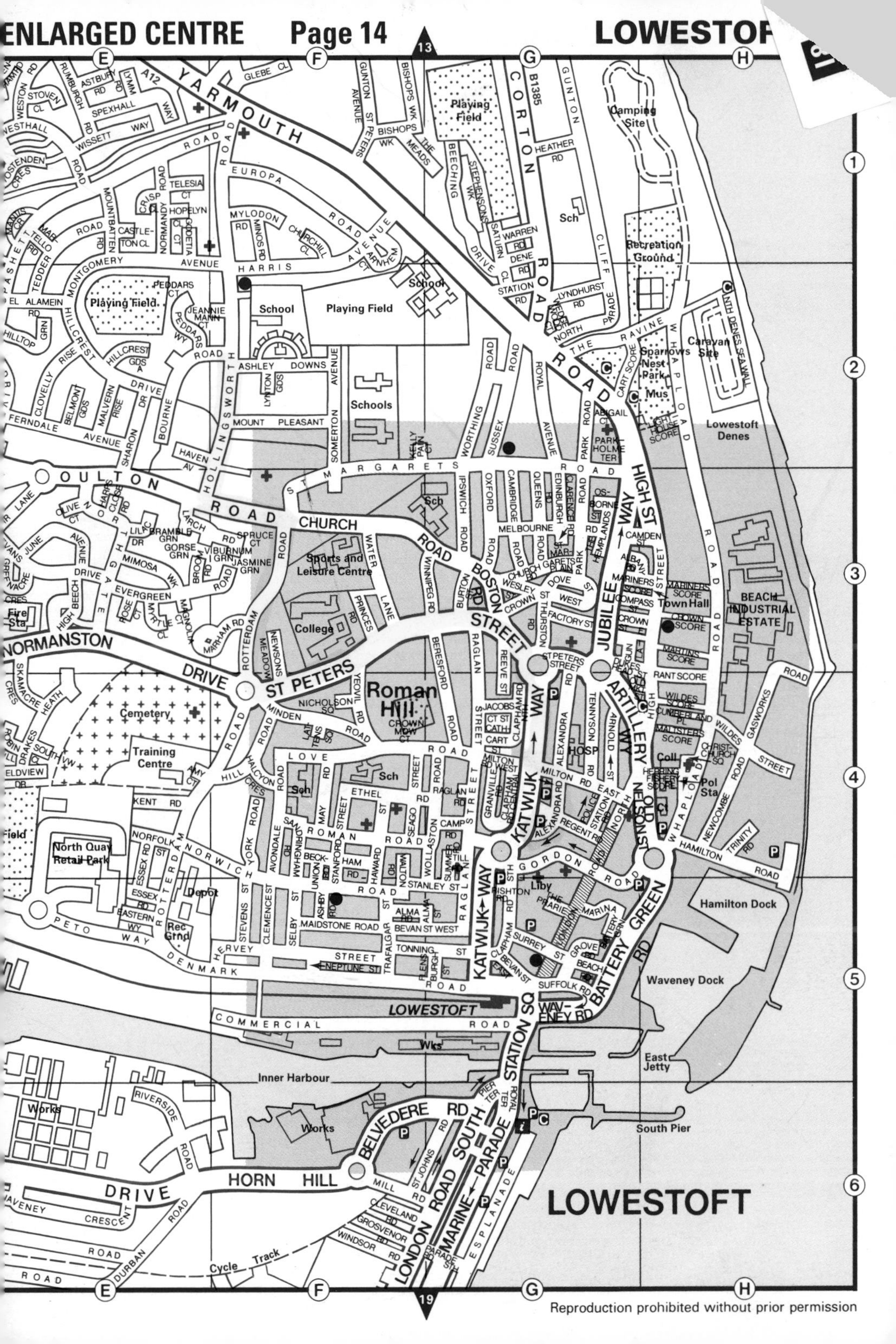
LOWESTOFT
Roman Hill
Inner Harbour
Hamilton Dock
Waveney Dock
South Pier
East Jetty
Lowestoft Denes
BEACH INDUSTRIAL ESTATE
North Quay Retail Park
Cemetery
Training Centre
Sports and Leisure Centre
College
Playing Field
Camping Site
Recreation Ground
Caravan Site
Sparrows Nest Park
Town Hall
YARMOUTH ROAD
OULTON ROAD
NORMANSTON DRIVE
ST PETERS STREET
CHURCH ROAD
HIGH ST
JUBILEE WAY
KATWIJK WAY
STATION SQ
COMMERCIAL ROAD
BELVEDERE RD
LONDON ROAD SOUTH
MARINE PARADE
ESPLANADE
HORN HILL
BATTERY GREEN RD
WHAPLOAD ROAD
DENMARK ROAD
CORTON ROAD

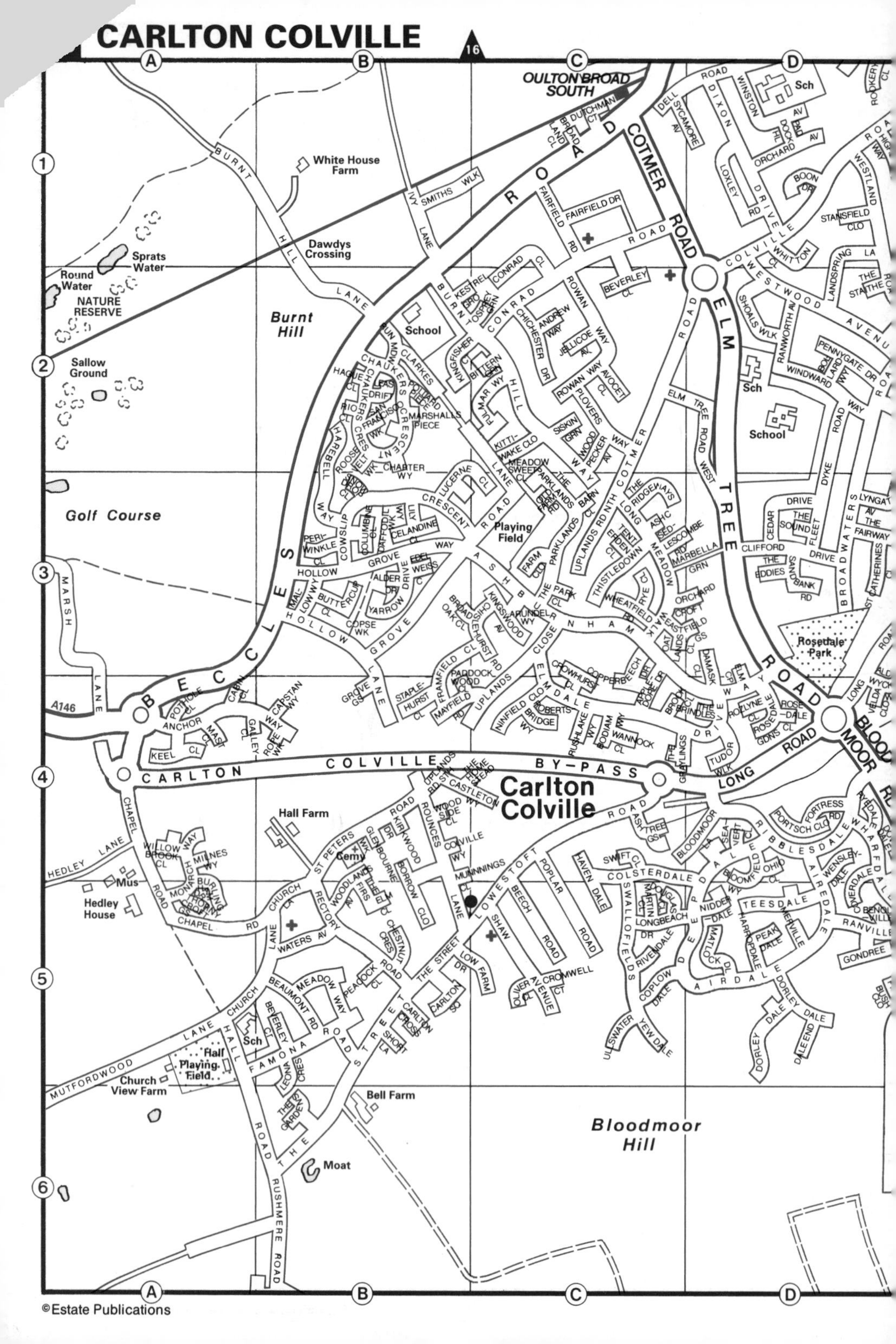
16
A
B
C
D
1
2
3
4
5
6
OULTON BROAD SOUTH
White House Farm
Dawdys Crossing
Sprats Water
Round Water
NATURE RESERVE
Sallow Ground
Burnt Hill
Golf Course
BURNT HILL LANE
BECCLES ROAD
COTMER ROAD
ELM TREE ROAD
MARSH LANE
A146
School
Sch
Playing Field
Rosedale Park
CARLTON COLVILLE BY-PASS
Carlton Colville
LONG ROAD
BLOODMOOR
Hall Farm
Cemy
Mus
Hedley House
HEDLEY LANE
CHAPEL ROAD
CHURCH LANE
MUTFORDWOOD LANE
Church View Farm
Hall Playing Field
Bell Farm
Moat
RUSHMERE ROAD
THE STREET
LOWESTOFT ROAD
Bloodmoor Hill
CHAUKERS CRESCENT
ASHBURNHAM WAY
ELMDALE DRIVE
COLSTERDALE
DEEPDALE
AIRDALE
RIBBLESDALE
WHARFDALE
BROADWATERS ROAD
UPLANDS ROAD
HOLLOW GROVE WAY
FAIRFIELD ROAD
COLVILLE ROAD
WESTWOOD AVENUE
SHAW AVENUE
POPLAR ROAD
BEECH ROAD
FAMONA ROAD

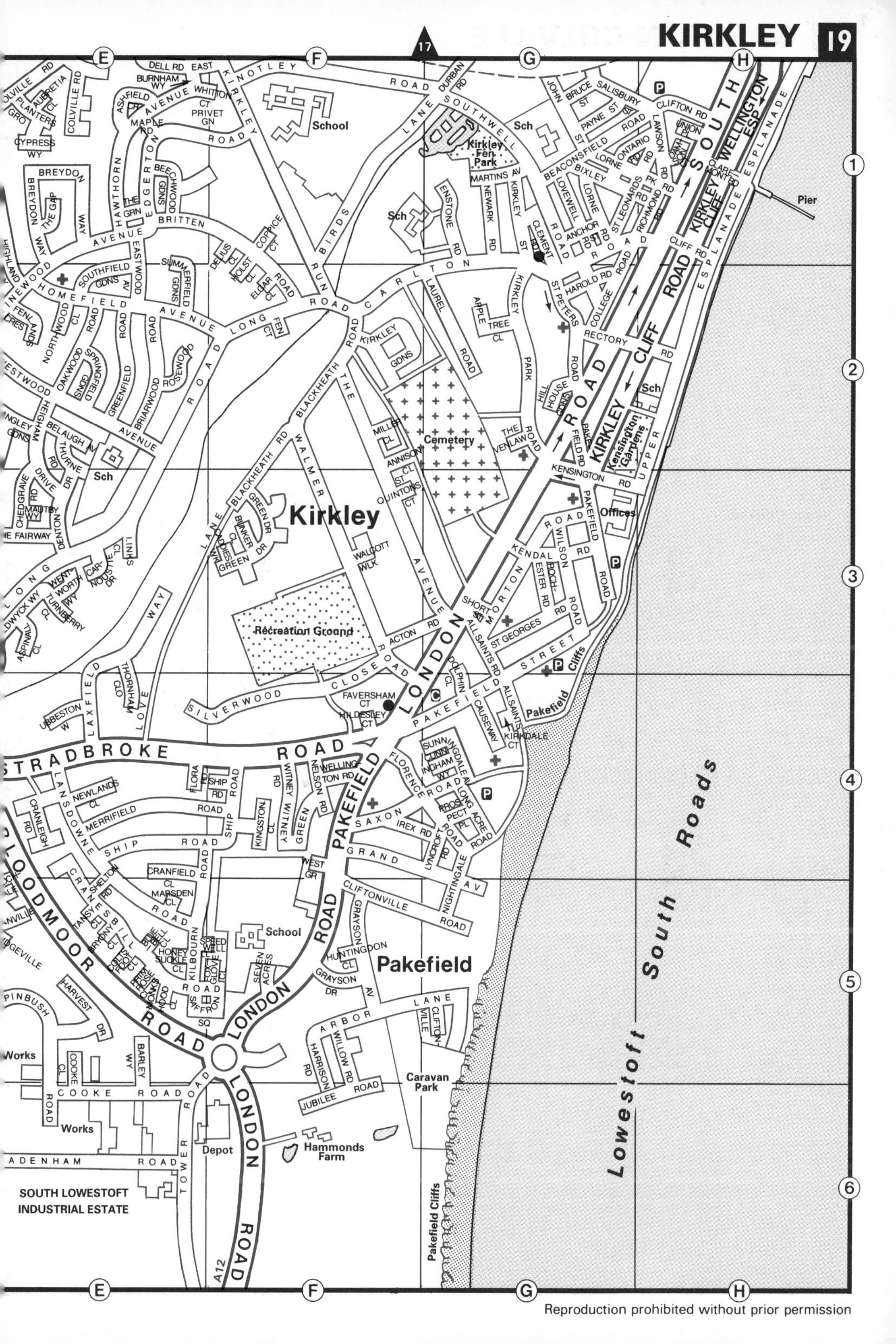
Kirkley
Pakefield
Lowestoft South Roads
Pier
School
Sch
Kirkley Fen Park
Cemetery
Recreation Ground
Offices
Cliffs
Pakefield Cliffs
Caravan Park
Hammonds Farm
Works
Depot
SOUTH LOWESTOFT INDUSTRIAL ESTATE
KIRKLEY CLIFF ROAD
SOUTH ESPLANADE
WELLINGTON ESP
LONDON ROAD
PAKEFIELD ROAD
STRADBROKE ROAD
BLOODMOOR ROAD
CARLTON ROAD
BRITTEN AVENUE
HOMEFIELD AVENUE
LONG ROAD
KIRKLEY RUN
NOTLEY ROAD
SOUTHWELL ROAD
KIRKLEY PARK ROAD
WALMER ROAD
THE AVENUE
BLACKHEATH RD
SILVERWOOD CLOSE
ACTON RD
PAKEFIELD STREET
KENSINGTON RD
CLIFFTONVILLE ROAD
GRAND AV
SAXON ROAD
LONG ACRE ROAD
NIGHTINGALE AV
ARBOR LANE
COOKE ROAD
ADENHAM ROAD
TOWER ROAD
A12
Reproduction prohibited without prior permission

The Index includes some names for which there is insufficient space on the maps. These names are preceded by an * and are followed by the nearest adjoining thoroughfare.

Empress Rd. NR31 7 E1
Englands La. NR31 9 G2
Erica Way. NR31 9 E1
Estcourt Rd. NR30 5 C5
Euston Rd. NR30 4 C1
Exeter Rd. NR31 9 F2
Exmouth Rd. NR30 4 B5

Factory Rd. NR30 4 C1
Falcon Ct. NR30 4 A1
Falkland Way. NR31 8 D3
Faraday Rd. NR31 7 E4
Farman Clo. NR31 10 C5
Fastolff Av. NR31 9 E4
Feathers Plain. NR31 9 G1
Fell Way. NR31 6 C5
Fellowes Dri. NR31 8 C2
Fenner Rd. NR30 7 G5
Fern Gdns. NR31 10 B6
Ferrier Clo. NR30 4 B1
Ferrier Rd. NR30 4 B1
Ferry Hill. NR31 7 G5
Ferry La. NR31 4 A4
Fisher Av. NR30 5 C3
Fishers Ct. NR30 4 B2
Fishers Quay. NR30 4 A2
Fitzalan Clo. NR30 4 A2
Forsythia Rd. NR31 9 E1
Foxglove Dri. NR31 8 C4
Foxs Pass. NR30 4 C3
Framlingham Clo. NR31 4 A5
Frank Stone Ct. NR30 4 C6
Frederick Rd. NR30 5 B5
Fremantle Rd. NR30 5 B1
Frederick Rd, Gorleston. NR31 7 F6
Friars La. NR30 4 B5
Fullers Hill. NR30 4 A1
Fulmar Clo. NR31 8 D1

Gainsborough Av. NR31 6 D6
Gapton Hall Rd. NR31 7 E4
Garfield Rd. NR30 5 C4
Garnham Rd. NR31 7 G6
Garrison Rd. NR30 5 B5
Gatacre Rd. NR31 7 E1
George St. NR30 4 A2
Girton Rd. NR31 9 E3
Gloucester Av. NR31 9 F3
Gonville Rd. NR31 9 E3
Gordon Rd. NR31 4 A5
Gordon Ter. NR30 4 C2
Gorleston La. NR31 8 C5
Gorse Clo. NR31 10 C2
Gournay Av. NR31 9 G4
Granta Way. NR31 9 E5
Granville Rd. NR31 7 E1
Great Northern Clo. NR30 5 C5
Grebe Clo. NR31 6 D6
Green La. NR31 8 B3
Greenacres. NR31 8 D4
Grenfell Ct. NR31 9 G3
Grenville Pl. NR30 5 C3
Gresham Clo. NR31 9 F4
Greyfriars Way. NR30 4 B3

Half Moon. NR31 9 F6
Hall Plain. NR30 4 B3
Hamilton Rd. NR30 5 B4
Hammond Rd. NR30 5 B5
Harbord Cres. NR30 7 G4
Harfreys Rd. NR31 7 E4
Harley Rd. NR30 5 C4
Harpers La. NR31 6 C4
Harry Miller Ct. NR30 4 C6
Hartman Rd. NR30 7 G6
Havelock Rd. NR30 4 C4
Hawkins Av. NR30 5 B2
Hawkins Clo. NR30 5 B3
Hawthorn Cres. NR31 8 C3
Hawthorn Rd. NR31 9 E1
Hazel Way. NR31 9 E1
Headington Clo. NR31 8 D2
Heath Grn. NR31 9 E1
Heather Gdns. NR31 10 B5
Heather Rd. NR31 10 B5
Heron Clo. NR31 6 D6
Herries Clo. NR30 4 A2
Hertford Way. NR31 9 E3
Hewett Clo. NR31 9 G4
Hewitt Rd. NR31 6 C5
Hickory Gdns. NR31 8 C2
High La. NR31 10 B1
High Mill Rd. NR31 7 E2
High Rd. NR31 7 F5
High St. NR31 9 G1
Highfield Rd. NR31 7 G5
Hill Av. NR31 9 G6
Hingley Clo. NR31 7 F5
Hobland La. NR31 8 C5
Hogarth Clo. NR31 6 D6
Holly Av. NR31 8 C2
Holly Way. NR31 9 E1
Homefield Av. NR31 8 C2
Hornbeam Clo. NR31 9 E1
Howard St Nth. NR30 4 A2
Howard St Sth. NR30 4 A2
Howe Rd. NR30 5 C4
Humber Keel. NR31 9 G6
Humberstone Rd. NR31 7 F6
Hunter Dri. NR31 6 C5

INDUSTRIAL & RETAIL:
Beacon Pk. NR31 9 E6
Enterprise Park. NR31 6 D4
Eurocentre Ind Est. NR30 5 A4
Gapton Hall Ind Est. NR31 6 C4
Gapton Retail Pk. NR31 7 E3
Harfreys Ind Est. NR31 7 E4
Marine Park. NR31 6 D4
St Nicholas Trading Est. NR30 5 C6
Yarmouth Business Pk. NR31 7 E3
Inner Relief Rd. NR31 7 F6
Isaacs Rd. NR31 7 E1
Isis Clo. NR31 9 E4
Ivy Grn. NR31 9 E1

James Watt Clo. NR31 6 D5
Jasmine Gdns. NR31 8 C1
Jasmine Grn. NR31 9 E1
Jellicoe Rd. NR30 5 B2
Jema Clo. NR30 5 B4
Jews La. NR31 8 C3
John Anderson Ct. NR31 8 D2
John Rd. NR31 9 G1
John Winter Ct. NR30 4 C1
Johns Av. NR31 9 E3
Johns Ter. NR30 4 C4
Jones Way. NR31 7 E2
Joshua Ct. NR31 9 G6
Jury St. NR30 4 C1

Kalmia Grn. NR31 9 E1
Keble Rd. NR31 9 E3
Kennedy Av. NR31 9 F6
Kent Av. NR31 9 F3
Kent Sq. NR30 4 C3
Keppel Rd. NR31 9 G2
Kestrel Clo. NR31 6 D6
Keyes Av. NR30 5 C3
Kimberley Ter. NR30 4 C5
King St. NR30 4 B1
Kingfisher Clo. NR31 6 C6
Kings Rd. NR30 4 C5
Kings Rd, Gorleston. NR31 9 E2
Kings Walk. NR31 9 E2
Kitchener Rd. NR30 5 B5

Laburnum Clo. NR31 8 C1
Laburnum Rd. NR31 9 E2
Lady Haven Rd. NR31 7 E1
Lady Margarets Av. NR31 9 E2
Lancaster Rd. NR30 4 C4
*Lancaster Sq, York Rd. N30 4 C3
Langham Rd. NR30 5 D6
Lapwing Clo. NR31 6 D6
Larch Dri. NR31 8 D2
Lark Way. NR31 8 D1
Laurel Dri. NR31 8 B2
Lawn Av. NR30 5 B5
Lawyer Corys. NR31 9 F6
Leach Clo. NR31 8 D3
Lefevre Way. NR31 6 C5
Leicester Rd. NR31 9 G2
Leman Rd. NR31 9 G5
Leys Clo. NR31 4 A6
Lichfield Rd. NR31 4 A4
Lilac Clo. NR31 8 D2
Lime Way. NR31 9 E1
*Limekiln Walk, Limekiln Way. NR30 4 A1
Limekiln Way. NR30 4 A1
Limmer Rd. NR31 9 G2
Lincoln Av. NR31 9 F4
Linden Tree Gdns. NR31 8 C2
Links Rd. NR31 9 F6
Linnet Clo. NR31 8 D1
Long La. NR31 8 D2
Lords La. NR31 8 A1
Louis Dahl Rd. NR31 10 C4
Louise Clo. NR30 4 C5
Lovewell Rd. NR31 9 F1
Lower Cliiff Rd. NR31 9 G3
Lower Esp. NR31 9 G3
Lowestoft Rd. NR31 9 F6
Lowry Clo. NR31 6 D5
Lucas Rd. NR31 7 E1
Lucerne Rd. NR31 8 C3
Lynn Gro. NR31 7 E6

Madden Av. NR30 5 C2
Magdalen Sq. NR31 9 E3
Magdalen St. NR31 9 E3
Magdalen Way. NR31 9 E3
Main Cross Rd. NR30 7 G5
Malakoff Clo. NR30 4 C4
Malakoff Rd. NR30 4 C4
Mallard Way. NR31 8 D1
Malthouse La. NR31 7 F5
Manby Rd. NR30 4 C2
Manby Rd, Gorleston. NR31 7 F5
Manor Clo. NR31 7 F5
Manor Rd. NR31 7 F5
Maple Gdns. NR31 8 C2
Marguerite Clo. NR31 8 C3
Marine Clo. NR31 9 G6
Marine Cres. NR30 5 C4
Marine Par. NR30 4 D5
Marine Par, Gorleston. NR31 9 G3
Mariners Clo. NR31 9 G6
Mariners Compass. NR31 9 F6
Mariners Rd. NR30 4 B5
Marjoram Rd. NR31 8 C4
Market Gates. NR30 4 B2
Market Rd. NR31 6 B6
Market Row. NR30 4 A2
*Marl Ter, Crown Rd. NR30 4 C3
Marlborough Ter. NR30 4 D3
Marsh La. NR31 10 B1
Marsh Rd. NR31 7 E2
Martin Clo. NR31 8 C1
Masquers Clo. NR31 9 G5
*Maud Ter, Belvidere Rd. NR30 5 C5
Maygrove Rd. NR30 5 C6
Meadow Ct. NR31 9 F6
Meadowland Dri. NR31 8 D3
Merton Av. NR31 9 E3
Micawber Av. NR30 7 G4
Middle Market Rd. NR30 4 B2
Middle Rd. NR30 7 G4
Middlegate. NR30 4 B4
Middlestone Clo. NR31 9 F3
Middleton Rd. NR31 9 F3
Midland Clo. NR30 5 C5
Mill La. NR31 6 C6
Mill La. NR31 8 C2
Mill Rd. NR31 7 E1
Mill Rd, Burgh Castle. NR31 10 C4
Mill Rd. NR31 6 A6
Milton Rd. NR30 5 C2
Minsmere Rd. NR31 10 B5
Moat Rd. NR30 5 C5
Monument Rd. NR30 7 H5
Moorland Way. NR31 10 C6
Morton Cres. NR31 8 C2
Morton Peto Rd. NR31 6 D5
Mulberry Gro. NR31 8 C3

Napoleon Pl. NR30 4 C4
Nelson Rd. NR31 9 G2
Nelson Rd Central. NR30 4 C2
Nelson Rd Nth. NR30 4 C2
Nelson Rd Sth. NR30 4 C5
New College Clo. NR31 9 E2
New Rd. NR31 10 B5
Newcastle Rd. NR30 4 B6
Newnham Grn. NR31 9 E3
Newton Cross. NR31 9 G6
Nile Rd. NR31 9 G3
Norfolk Sq. NR30 5 C6
Norman La. NR31 6 D5
North Denes Rd. NR30 5 C4
North Dri. NR30 4 D2
North Market Rd. NR30 4 B2
North Quay. NR30 4 A2
North River Rd. NR30 5 B5
North Rd. NR31 9 G3
Northgate St. NR30 5 B4
Nottingham Way. NR30 4 B4
Nuffield Cres. NR31 9 E3
Nuffield Clo. NR31 9 E3
Nursery Clo. NR31 10 C6
Nursery Ter. NR30 5 B5

Oak Av. NR31 8 C2
Oak Rd. NR31 9 E1
Old Fountain. NR31 9 F6
*Old Wellington Pl, Duncan Rd. NR30 4 C4
Olive Rd. NR31 7 E1
Oliver Ct. NR31 4 A6
Onslow Av. NR30 5 C3
Orde Av. NR31 9 F5
Orford Clo. NR30 4 B4
Oriel Av. NR31 8 D4
Oriel Way. NR31 9 E4
Ormond Rd. NR30 5 B5
Orwell Cres. NR31 10 B5
Osborne Av. NR30 5 B4
Owen Rd. NR31 7 E4
Oxford Av. NR31 9 E4

Paddock Clo. NR31 10 B5
Paddys Loke. NR30 5 A4
Paget Rd. NR30 4 C2
Palgrave Rd. NR30 5 B5
Palmer Rd. NR31 9 G1
Park Rd. NR31 9 G4
Parkland Dri. NR31 8 D2
Pasteur Rd. NR31 7 E3
Paston Pl. NR30 4 C3
Paston Rd. NR31 9 F2
Patterson Clo. NR30 4 A2
Pattinsons Rd. NR30 5 A4
Pavilion Rd. NR31 9 G2
Peggotty Rd. NR30 7 G4
Pembroke Av. NR31 9 E3
Perebrown Av. NR30 5 C3
Peterhouse Av. NR31 9 F3
Pier Gdns. NR31 9 G3
Pier Pl. NR30 4 C5
Pier Plain. NR31 9 G2
Pier Rd. NR31 9 G3
Pier Walk. NR31 9 G2
Pine Grn. NR31 9 E2
Pinecot Av. NR31 8 C3
Pintail Dri. NR31 8 D1
Plane Rd. NR31 7 F6
Plevna Ter. NR31 4 A3
Plover Clo. NR31 6 D6
Pommers La. NR30 7 G5
Poplar Av. NR31 9 F3
Porters Loke. NR31 10 A4
Portland Ct. NR31 4 A4
Portland La. NR31 4 A4
Portland Pl. NR30 4 C4
Potters Field. NR31 9 E5
Pound La. NR31 9 F4
Primrose Way. NR31 8 C3
Princes Rd. NR30 4 C2
Priory Gdns. NR30 4 B1
Priory Plain. NR30 4 B1
Priory St. NR31 7 G6
Provan Cres. NR31 10 C6

Quay Angel. NR31 9 G6
Quay Mill Walk. NR30 4 A2
Quay Ostend. NR31 9 F6
Quay Rd. NR31 9 G2
Queen Annes Rd. NR31 7 F4
Queen St. NR30 4 B3
Queens Cres. NR31 9 F3
Queens Rd. NR30 4 B5
*Queens Sq, Albion Rd. NR30 4 C2

Raleigh Av. NR30 5 C3
Rambouillet Clo. NR31 8 D2
Rampart Rd. NR30 5 B6
Ranworth Clo. NR31 10 C5
Raven Clo. NR31 6 D6
Recreation Clo. NR31 9 F1
Recreation Rd. NR31 9 F1
Redwing Dri. NR31 6 D6
Regent Rd. NR30 4 B2
Regent St. NR30 4 A3
River Walk. NR30 5 B3
River Way. NR31 10 A4
Riverside Rd. NR31 7 G5
Riverside Walk. NR31 9 G1
Robin Clo. NR31 8 D1
Rodney Rd. NR30 4 C3
Roman Pl. NR30 4 C2
Rosedale Gdns. NR31 10 B6
Roseview Clo. NR31 8 C3
Roslyn Rd. NR31 9 F2
Rowan Clo. NR31 8 C1
Rowan Way. NR31 9 E1
Royal Av. NR30 5 C3
Runham Rd. NR30 5 A5
Ruskin Av. NR31 9 E4
Russell Av. NR31 9 F4
Russell Rd. NR30 4 C3

Sackville Clo. NR30 4 B3
St Andrews Clo. NR31 9 F2
St Andrews Rd. NR31 9 F1
St Annes Cres. NR31 9 E2
St Annes Cres. NR31 9 E3
St Annes Way. NR31 10 C5
St Antonys Av. NR31 9 E4
St Benets Rd. NR31 9 E3
St Catherines Way. NR31 9 E3
St Christopher Clo. NR31 10 C5
St Davids Clo. NR31 10 C5
St Edmund Clo. NR31 9 E4
St Francis Way. NR30 4 A2
St Furseys Way. NR31 10 C4
*St Georges Pl, King St. NR30 4 B3
St Georges Rd. NR30 4 C3
St Georges Rd, Belton. NR31 10 C5
St Hildas Cres. NR31 9 F2
St Hughs Grn. NR31 9 E4
St James Cres. NR31 10 C5
*St James Walk, York Rd. NR30 4 C3
St Johns Rd. NR31 10 B5
St Lukes Ter. NR31 7 E1
St Marys Ct. NR30 4 C2
St Marys La. NR31 4 A4
St Nicholas Ct. NR31 8 B2
St Nicholas Gdns. NR31 8 B3
St Nicholas Rd. NR30 4 B2
St Pauls Way. NR30 5 B4
St Peters Av. NR31 9 E4
St Peters Ct. NR30 4 C4
St Peters Plain. NR30 4 C3
St Peters Rd. NR30 4 C4
St Roberts Way. NR31 10 C5
Salisbury Rd. NR30 5 C4
Salmon Rd. NR30 7 G5
Sam Brown Ct. NR31 8 D2
Sandown Rd. NR30 5 C5
Sandpiper Clo. NR31 8 D1
Sandringham Av. NR30 5 C3
Sandy La, Belton. NR31 10 B6
Sandy La, Bradwell. NR31 6 B5
*Sarah Martin Row, Howard St. NR30 4 A2
Sawmill La. NR31 7 E1
Saxon Rd. NR30 4 C3
School La. NR31 9 G1
School Rd. NR30 5 B5
School Rd Back. NR30 5 B6
Seafield Clo. NR30 4 C5
Seawake Clo. NR31 9 E2
Sefton La. NR31 4 A4
Selby Pl. NR30 4 B5
Selwyn Dri. NR31 10 C6
Selwyn Rd. NR31 8 D2
Seymour Av. NR30 5 C3
Shadingfield Clo. NR30 4 C5
Shakespeare Rd. NR30 5 D3
Sharmans Loke. NR31 10 B5
Shearwater Dri. NR31 6 D5
*Sheldonian Ct, Oriel Av. NR31 8 D3
Shire Av. NR31 6 C5
Shrublands Way. NR31 9 E1

Shuttleworth Clo. NR31 6 D5
Sidney Clo. NR30 4 B4
Silkmill Rd. NR30 4 B2
Silver Gdns. NR31 10 C6
Sinclair Ct. NR31 7 E5
Siskin Clo. NR31 8 D1
Smiths Loke. NR31 8 D1
Snowdrop Clo. NR31 8 D4
*Somerset Pl,
  Russell Rd. NR31 4 C3
Somerville Av. NR31 9 E4
Sorrel Rd. NR31 8 C4
South Beach Par. NR30 4 C4
South Denes Rd. NR30 7 G4
South Gdn. NR31 9 F6
South Market Rd. NR30 4 B2
South Quay. NR30 4 A3
South Rd. NR30 5 D2
South Rd,
  Gorleston. NR31 9 G3
*Southampton Pl,
  Princes Rd. NR30 4 C2
Southgates Rd. NR30 4 B5
Southtown Rd. NR31 4 A3
Sparrow Rd. NR31 8 C1
Spencer Av. NR31 9 F1
Spens Av. NR31 9 E4
Springfield Rd. NR31 9 G3
Stafford Rd. NR31 7 E2
Standard Pl. NR30 4 C4
Standard Rd. NR30 4 D3
Stanley Av. NR31 9 F4
Stanley Rd. NR30 5 B5
Stanley Ter. NR30 4 C2
Star Farm Clo. NR31 8 C2
Station Rd. NR31 7 E2
Station Rd Nth. NR31 10 B5
Station Rd Sth. NR31 10 B6
Steam Mill La. NR31 7 F1
Stephenson Clo. NR31 5 C5
Stepshort. NR31 10 C4
Stone Rd. NR31 7 E1
Stonecutters Way. NR30 4 A2
Stradbroke Rd. NR31 9 F2
Stuart Clo. NR31 9 E2
Sturdee Av. NR31 5 C3
Styles Clo. NR31 8 D3
Suffield Rd. NR31 9 F2
Suffling Rd. NR30 7 G5
Suffolk Clo. NR31 7 F5
Suffolk Pl. NR30 4 C2
Suffolk Rd. NR31 7 F3
Sun La. NR31 8 C2
Sunninghill Clo. NR31 6 C6
Sussex Rd. NR31 9 G2
Sutton Rd. NR30 7 G4
Swallow Clo. NR31 8 D6
Swanston Rd. NR30 7 G4
Swirles Pl. NR30 4 B2
Sycamore Av. NR31 8 C2
Sycamore Grn. NR31 9 E1

Tamworth La. NR31 7 E2
Tar Works Rd. NR30 5 B4
Temple Rd. NR30 4 B2
Tennyson Rd. NR30 5 C3
Tern Gdns. NR31 8 D1
Thamesfield Way. NR31 7 E3
The Boulters. NR31 9 F6
The Buntings. NR31 6 D6
The Close. NR31 8 D2
The Conge. NR30 4 A1
The Fairway. NR31 9 G6
The Glebes. NR31 10 B5
The Green. NR31 10 C6
The Lawns. NR31 5 B4
The Loke. NR31 10 A5
The Mews. NR31 9 F6
The Naze. NR31 10 C5
The Orchards. NR31 10 C5
The Pastures. NR31 7 E6
The Staithe. NR31 10 C5
The Street. NR30 5 D1
The Walk. NR31 7 E6
The Willows. NR31 8 D4
Theatre Plain. NR30 4 B2
Tolhouse St. NR30 4 B3
Tollgate Rd. NR31 4 A6
Tottenham St. NR30 4 C1
Town Wall Rd. NR30 5 B6
Townlands. NR31 7 E6
Townsend Clo. NR30 4 B3
*Trafalgar Ct,
  Trafalgar Rd. NR30 4 C3
Trafalgar Rd. NR30 4 C3

Trafalgar Rd East.
  NR31 7 G6
Trafalgar Rd West.
  NR31 7 F6
Trafalgar Sq. NR30 4 D3
Trinity Av. NR31 9 E2
*Trinity Pl,
  Alma Rd. NR30 4 C4
Tudor Walk. NR31 9 F5
Turner Bank Row.
  NR30 4 A2
Turner Clo. NR31 6 D6
Tyrrells Rd. NR31 7 E1

Union Rd. NR30 4 C2
University Cres. NR31 9 E2
Upper Cliff Rd. NR31 9 G3
Upper Esp. NR31 9 G3

Vanguard Rd. NR31 6 D5
Vauxhall Ter. NR30 5 B5
Veronica Grn. NR31 9 E1
Vervain Clo. NR31 8 C3
Victoria Pl. NR30 4 C4
Victoria Rd. NR30 4 C4
Victoria Rd,
  Gorleston. NR31 9 G4
Victoria St. NR30 5 C5
Viking Av. NR31 9 G4
Viking Rd. NR31 6 C5
Violet Clo. NR31 8 D3

Wadham Clo. NR31 9 F4
Wadham Rd. NR31 9 F4
Wagtail Clo. NR31 6 D6
Walpole Rd. NR30 5 C4
Warbler Clo. NR31 8 D1
Warren Rd. NR31 9 G6
Waunci Cres. NR31 9 G5
Waveney Dri. NR31 10 C5
Waveney Rd. NR31 7 F4
Wedgewood Clo. NR31 9 F4
Well Rd. NR30 4 C4
Well St. NR30 4 C1
Wellesley Rd. NR30 4 C1
Wellington Pl. NR30 4 B3
Wellington Rd. NR30 4 C4
Wensum Way. NR31 10 C5
West Av. NR31 9 F4
West Rd. NR30 5 D1
Westbrook Av. NR31 9 E1
Western By-Pass.
  NR30 5 A6
Western Rd. NR31 9 F2
Wherry Way. NR30 5 B4
Whinchat Way. NR31 8 D1
White Clover Rd. NR31 8 C4
White Horse Plain.
  NR30 4 B1
Widgeon Clo. NR31 8 D1
Willow Av. NR31 8 C1
Wilshere Ct. NR30 4 C4
Windsor Av. NR30 5 C3
Windsor Way. NR31 9 E3
Winifred Rd. NR31 7 E1
Wolseley Rd. NR31 7 F2
Woodcock Mews. NR31 6 D6
Woodfarm La. NR31 8 D4
Woodpecker Mews.
  NR31 8 D1
Worcester Way. NR31 9 E2
Wren Dri. NR31 6 D6

Yallop Av. NR31 9 G6
Yare Clo. NR30 5 B5
Yare Rd. NR31 10 C5
Yarmouth Way. NR30 4 B3
Yaxley Rd. NR30 5 A5
Yew Tree Clo. NR31 8 B2
York Rd. NR30 4 C3
Youell Av. NR31 9 G5

HOPTON-ON-SEA

Anglian Way. NR31 11 B4
Barn Clo. NR31 11 C4
Beach Clo. NR31 11 C5
Boyton La. NR31 11 B5
Bishops Walk. NR31 11 B4
Brotherton Way. NR31 11 B4
Cadiz Way. NR31 11 C4
Coast Rd. NR31 11 B4
Culley Way. NR31 11 B4
Cumby Way. NR31 11 B4

Dorking Rd. NR31 11 A4
Flowerday Clo. NR31 11 B3
Freeman Clo. NR31 11 B4
Geneva Gdns. NR31 11 C4
Groomes Clo. NR31 11 B4
Gurney Clo. NR31 11 B4
Hall Rd. NR31 11 A4
Hobbs Way. NR31 11 B5
Hopton By-Pass. NR31 11 A1
Hopton Gdns. NR31 11 B4
Imperial Mews. NR31 11 B4
Ives Way. NR31 11 B4
Jay La. NR31 11 A5
Jex Way. NR31 11 B4
Julian Way. NR31 11 B4
Kidds Clo. NR31 11 B5
Longfulans La. NR31 11 B4
Lowestoft Rd. NR31 11 B4
*Lushers Meadow Way,
  Seafields Dri. NR31 11 C4
Manor Gdns. NR31 11 C4
Manor Rd. NR31 11 C5
Mariners Park Clo.
  NR31 11 B4
Misburgh Way. NR31 11 C4
Naples Clo. NR31 11 C4
Newton Gap Clo. NR31 11 B4
Noel Clo. NR31 11 B3
Old Church Rd. NR31 11 B4
Ormsby Way. NR31 11 B4
Pebble View Wk.
  NR31 11 C4
Potters Dri. NR31 11 B3
Rackham Clo. NR31 11 B3
Randall Clo. NR31 11 B3
Rogers Clo. NR31 11 B4
St Andrew Ct. NR31 11 C4
St Clare Ct. NR31 11 C4
St Clement Mws.
  NR31 11 B4
St Margarets Way.
  NR31 11 B3
St Vincent Wk. NR31 11 C4
Sands Clo. NR31 11 C4
Sayers Grn. NR31 11 B4
Seafields Dri. NR31 11 B4
Sea View Rise. NR31 11 C5
Station Rd. NR31 11 B4
Suffolk Clo. NR31 11 B4
The Laurels. NR31 11 B5
Turin Way. NR31 11 C4
Walters Clo. NR31 11 B4
Warren Rd. NR31 11 B1
Watsons Clo. NR31 11 C4
White Clover Way.
  NR31 11 B5
Zurich Clo. NR31 11 C4

LOWESTOFT

Abigail Ct. NR32 17 G2
Acton Rd. NR33 19 F3
*Adrian Rd,
  Alexandra Rd. NR32 17 G4
Airedale. NR33 18 D5
Airey Clo. NR32 12 D6
Akethorpe Way. NR32 16 D2
Albany Rd. NR32 14 C2
Alder Dri. NR32 18 B3
Aldwych Way. NR33 18 B4
Alexandra Rd. NR32 14 C3
All Saints Rd. NR33 19 G3
Allen Rd. NR32 15 D4
Allington Smith Clo.
  NR32 12 C6
Alma Rd. NR32 14 A5
Alma St. NR32 14 B5
Amberley Ct. NR32 16 C2
Amy Ct. NR32 17 E4
Anchor St. NR33 19 G1
Andrew Way. NR32 18 C2
Annison Clo. NR33 19 F3
Apple Tree Clo. NR32 19 G2
Appledore Dri. NR33 18 C3
Arbor La. NR33 19 F5
Arnhem Ct. NR32 17 F1
Arnold St. NR32 14 C3
Artillery Way. NR32 14 C3
Arundel Way. NR33 18 C3
Ash Clo. NR32 18 C3
Ashburnham Way.
  NR33 18 C3
Ashby Rd. NR32 14 A5

Ashfield Cres. NR33 19 E1
Ashley Downs. NR32 17 F2
Ashness Pk. NR32 16 D1
Ashtree Gdns. NR33 18 C4
Aspen Coppice. NR32 12 D6
Aspinall Clo. NR33 19 E3
Astbury Rd. NR32 17 E1
Aubretia Clo. NR33 19 E1
Avocet Clo. NR33 18 C2
Avondale Rd. NR32 17 F4

Barkis Mdw. NR32 12 B2
Barley Way. NR33 19 E5
Barn Clo. NR33 18 C3
Battery Grn. NR32 14 C5
Battery Grn Rd. NR32 14 C5
Beach Rd. NR32 18 C3
Beaconsfield Rd. NR33 19 G1
Beaumont Rd. NR33 18 D3
Beccles Rd. NR33 18 A4
Beckham Rd. NR32 14 A4
Beech Rd. NR33 18 C5
Beeching Dri. NR32 17 G1
Beechwood Gdns.
  NR33 19 E1
Belaugh Av. NR33 19 E1
Belle Vue Clo. NR32 14 C1
Belmont Gdns. NR32 17 E2
Belvedere Rd. NR33 17 F6
Benouville. NR33 18 B5
Bentley Dri. NR33 13 E6
Beresford Rd. NR32 14 B2
Berkeley Gdns. NR32 16 D2
Berry Clo. NR32 16 B4
Bevan St East. NR32 14 B5
Bevan St West. NR32 14 A5
Beverley Clo. NR33 18 B5
Beverley Ct. NR33 18 B5
Birch Clo. NR32 15 D3
Birds La. NR33 19 F1
Bishops Wk. NR32 17 F1
Bittern Grn. NR33 18 C2
Bixley Rd. NR33 19 G1
Blackberry Way. NR32 16 C3
Blackheath Rd. NR33 19 F2
Blakenham Clo. NR32 16 C2
Blinco Rd. NR32 15 C4
Bloodmoor La. NR33 18 D4
Bloodmoor Rd. NR33 18 D4
Bloomfield Way. NR33 18 D4
Bloomsbury Clo.
  NR32 14 B4
Bluebell Clo. NR33 19 E5
Blundeston Marsh La.
  NR32 12 A4
Blundeston Rd. NR32 12 D3
Blyford Rd. NR32 13 E6
Boathouse La. NR32 15 B5
Bodiam Way. NR33 18 C4
Bollard Way. NR33 18 D2
Bon Marche. NR32 14 C5
Bonds Mdw. NR32 16 C4
Boon Dri. NR33 18 D1
Borrow Clo. NR33 18 B5
Borrow Rd. NR32 15 C5
Bosquet Clo. NR32 12 D6
Boston Rd. NR32 14 C2
Bourne Rd. NR32 17 E2
Bramble Grn. NR32 17 E3
Bramfield Rd. NR32 16 D2
Breckland Way. NR32 16 D2
Brendon Way. NR32 16 B3
Breydon Way. NR33 19 E1
Briar Clo. NR32 13 E6
Briarwood Rd. NR33 19 E5
Bridge Rd. NR33 18 B6
Britten Rd. NR33 19 E1
Broad Oak Clo. NR33 18 C3
Broad Rd. NR32 15 D4
Broad View Rd. NR32 15 C5
Broadfleet Clo. NR32 16 B1
Broadland Rd. NR33 18 C1
Broadwaters Rd. NR33 18 D3
Brook Clo. NR33 18 C4
Broom Rd. NR32 17 E3
Bruce St. NR33 19 G1
Bryony Clo. NR33 19 E5
Bunker Clo. NR33 19 F3
Burgess Clo. NR32 16 C4
Burlingham Dri. NR33 18 A5
Burnham Way. NR32 16 D6
Burnt Hill La. NR33 18 B3
Burnt Hill Way. NR33 18 B2
Burton St. NR32 14 B2
Burwood Way. NR33 13 F6
Butley Dri. NR32 16 D2

Buttercup Clo. NR33 18 B3

Cabin Clo. NR33 18 A4
Caddies Wk. NR33 19 F3
Caldecott Rd. NR32 14 B1
Cambrian Cres. NR32 16 B3
Cambridge Rd. NR32 14 B1
Camden St. NR32 14 C1
Camp Rd. NR32 14 B4
Canaletto Clo. NR32 13 F5
Capstan Way. NR33 18 B4
Carlton Colville
  By-Pass. NR33 18 A4
Carlton Cross. NR33 18 B5
Carlton Rd. NR33 19 F2
Carlton Sq. NR33 19 F2
Carnoustie Dri. NR33 19 E3
Cart Score. NR32 17 G2
Castleton Av. NR33 17 E1
Castleton Way. NR33 18 B4
Cathcart St. NR32 14 B3
Causeway. NR33 19 G4
Cavendish Clo. NR32 16 D3
Cedar Dri. NR33 18 D3
Celandine Clo. NR33 18 B3
Chapel Ct. NR32 14 C2
Chapel Rd. NR33 18 A4
Charter Way. NR33 18 B2
Chatsworth Clo. NR32 16 D2
Chaukers Cres. NR33 18 B2
Chedgrave Rd. NR33 19 E3
Chestnut Av. NR32 16 B4
Chestnut Cres. NR33 18 B5
Cheviot Rd. NR32 15 D3
Chichester Dri. NR33 18 C2
Chiltern Cres. NR32 16 B3
Chislehurst Rd. NR33 18 C3
*Christchurch Sq,
  Whapload Rd. NR32 14 D3
Christmas La. NR32 15 C4
Church Av. NR32 15 C4
Church La, Carlton
  Colville. NR33 18 B5
Church La,
  Corton. NR32 13 F1
Church La,
  Oulton. NR32 15 C4
Church Rd,
  Blundeston. NR32 12 A3
Church Rd,
  Lowestoft. NR32 14 A1
Churchill Clo. NR32 17 F1
Clapham Rd Central.
  NR32 14 B4
Clapham Rd Nth. NR32 14 B3
Clapham Rd Sth. NR32 14 B5
Claremont Rd. NR33 19 H1
Clarence Rd. NR32 14 C1
Clarkes La. NR33 18 B2
Clarkson Rd. NR32 15 C4
Claydon Dri. NR32 16 C2
Clemence St. NR32 17 F5
Clement Rd. NR33 19 G1
Cleveland Rd. NR33 17 F6
Cliff Rd. NR33 19 H1
Clifford Dri. NR33 18 D3
Clifton Rd. NR33 19 H1
Cliftonville. NR33 19 G5
Cliftonville Rd. NR33 19 F5
Clovelly Rise. NR32 17 E2
Clover Way. NR33 13 G6
College Mdws. NR32 16 D2
College Rd. NR33 19 G2
Colman Rd. NR32 13 F2
Colsterdale. NR33 18 C4
Coltsfoot Clo. NR33 19 E5
Columbine Clo. NR33 18 B3
Colville Rd. NR33 18 D1
Colville Way. NR33 18 B4
Commercial Rd. NR32 14 A6
Commodore Rd. NR32 16 B4
Compass St. NR32 14 C2
Conrad Clo. NR33 18 C2
Conrad Rd. NR32 18 C2
Constable Clo. NR33 18 C2
Cooke Clo. NR33 19 E5
Cooke Rd. NR33 19 E6
Coplow Dale. NR33 18 C5
Copperbeach Dri. NR33 18 C3
Coppice La. NR32 19 F1
Copse Wk. NR33 18 B3
Corton Long La. NR33 13 G3
Corton Rd. NR32 13 G3
Cotman Clo. NR33 13 F5
Cotmer Rd. NR33 18 C1
Cotswold Way. NR32 16 B3

Street	Map Ref
Coverdale. NR33	18 D5
Cowslip Cres. NR33	18 B3
Cranesbill Rd. NR33	19 E5
Cranfield Clo. NR33	19 E4
Cranleigh Rd. NR33	19 E4
Cranworth Gdns. NR32	16 C2
Crestview Dri. NR32	16 D2
Crisp Clo. NR32	17 E1
Crompton Rd. NR33	16 C6
Crome Walk. NR32	13 F6
Cromwell Ct. NR33	18 C5
Cross Keys. NR32	14 B2
Crowhurst Clo. NR33	18 C3
Crown Meadow Ct. NR32	14 B3
Crown Score. NR32	14 D2
Crown St East. NR32	14 C2
Crown St West. NR32	14 B2
Culzean Gdns. NR32	16 D1
Cumberland Pl. NR32	14 D3
Cunningham Way. NR33	19 G4
Curlew Grn. NR32	15 C4
Cutler Ct. NR32	15 C3
Cutler Rd. NR32	15 C3
Cypress Way. NR33	19 E1
Daffodil Wk. NR33	18 B3
Dale End. NR33	18 D5
Damask Clo. NR33	18 D3
Damson Ct. NR33	19 H1
Darsham Vale. NR32	16 C1
Dawson Mews. NR32	13 E6
Debham Dri. NR32	16 C2
Deepdale. NR33	18 D5
Degas Gdns. NR32	13 F5
Delius Clo. NR33	19 F1
Dell Ct. NR33	16 C6
Dell Rd. NR33	16 B6
Dell Rd East. NR33	16 C6
Dene Rd. NR32	17 G1
Denmark Rd. NR32	14 A5
Denton Dri. NR33	19 E3
Derwent Gdns. NR32	16 D2
Desmond Clo. NR32	15 D4
Dickens Ct. NR32	12 A3
Diprose Way. NR32	13 E6
Dixon Dri. NR33	18 D1
Dolphin Clo. NR33	19 G4
Dorley Dale. NR33	18 D5
Douglas Clo. NR33	18 C5
Dove St. NR32	14 C2
Dovedale. NR33	18 D4
Drakes Heath. NR32	17 E4
Dukes Head St. NR32	14 C2
Dunston Dri. NR32	16 B2
Dunwich Way. NR32	16 C2
Durban Rd. NR33	17 C6
Dutchman Ct. NR33	18 C1
Eastern Way. NR32	17 E5
Eastfield Gdns. NR33	18 C3
Eastwood Av. NR33	19 E2
Edelweiss Clo. NR33	18 B3
Edendale. NR32	15 D4
Edgerton Rd. NR33	19 E1
Edinburgh Rd. NR32	14 C1
El Alamein Rd. NR32	17 E2
Elgar Clo. NR33	19 F2
Elizabeth Clo. NR32	16 D3
Elm Clo. NR33	18 B5
Elm Coppice. NR33	18 D4
Elm Tree Rd. NR33	18 D2
Elm Tree Rd West. NR33	18 D2
Elmdale Dri. NR33	18 C4
Elmhurst Av. NR32	16 B4
Enstone Rd. NR33	19 G1
Eskdale Way. NR32	16 D1
Esplanade. NR33	17 G6
Essex Rd. NR32	17 E4
Ethel Rd. NR32	14 A3
Europa Rd. NR32	17 F1
Evans Dri. NR32	17 E3
Evergreen Rd. NR32	17 E3
Everitt Ct. NR32	16 A5
Everitt Rd. NR33	16 B6
Factory St. NR32	14 C2
Fairfield Dri. NR33	18 C1
Fairfield Rd. NR33	18 C1
Fallowfields. NR32	12 D6
Famona Rd. NR33	18 B5
Farm Clo. NR33	18 C3
Farnham Clo. NR32	16 C2
Fastolf Clo. NR32	16 D2
Faversham Ct. NR33	19 F4
Fen Ct. NR33	19 F2
Fenlands Cres. NR33	19 E2
Fern Av. NR32	15 D4
Fern Green Clo. NR32	16 B2
Ferndale Av. NR32	17 E2
Fieldview Dri. NR32	17 E4
Fir La. NR32	16 D3
Fisher Row. NR32	15 B5
Fiske Gdns. NR32	16 C1
Fleet Dyke Rd. NR33	18 D3
Flensburgh St. NR32	14 B5
Flixton Marsh La. NR32	12 A5
Flixton Rd. NR32	12 A1
Flora Rd. NR33	19 E4
Florence Rd. NR33	19 F4
Fortress Rd. NR33	18 D4
Four Ways La. NR32	12 A1
Fowlers Cres. NR32	13 G2
Fox Glade. NR32	16 A4
Foxborough Rd. NR32	16 D1
Foxburrow Hill. NR32	13 E5
Foxes Walk. NR32	13 E5
Foxglove Clo. NR33	15 C4
Framfield Clo. NR33	18 B4
Fritton Clo. NR32	16 C2
Frostenden Cres. NR32	17 E1
Fulmar Way. NR33	18 C2
Fyffe Way. NR33	14 B6
Gainsborough Dri. NR32	13 F5
Galley Clo. NR33	18 A4
Gasworks Rd. NR32	14 D3
Gilpin Rd. NR32	15 D4
Gladstone Rd. NR32	13 F2
Glebe Clo. NR32	17 F1
Glemsford Rd. NR32	16 C2
Glenbourne Wk. NR33	18 B4
Gloucester Av. NR32	16 C2
Godetia Ct. NR32	17 E1
Gondree. NR33	18 D5
Gordon Rd. NR32	24 B4
Gorleston Rd. NR32	16 C4
Gorse Grn. NR32	17 E3
Grampian Way. NR32	15 D3
Grand Av. NR33	19 F4
Grange Rd. NR32	15 D3
Granville Rd. NR32	14 B4
Gravel Dam. NR32	15 A3
Grayson Av. NR33	19 F5
Grayson Dri. NR33	19 F5
Green Dri. NR33	19 F3
Green Fleet Dri. NR32	16 B2
Greenacre Cres. NR32	17 E3
Greenfield Rd. NR33	19 E2
Greenwood Way. NR32	13 E5
Gresham Av. NR32	16 C3
Gresham Clo. NR32	16 C3
Grosvenor Rd. NR33	17 F6
Grove Gdns. NR33	18 B4
Grove Rd. NR32	14 C5
Grove Rd, Carlton Colville. NR33	18 B3
Gun La. NR32	14 C2
Gunton Av. NR32	13 E4
Gunton Church La. NR32	13 G6
Gunton Cliff. NR32	17 G1
Gunton Dri. NR32	13 H6
Gunton St Peters Av. NR32	17 F1
Guscott Clo. NR32	13 E6
Hadenham Rd. NR33	19 E6
Hadleigh Dri. NR32	16 C3
Hague Clo. NR33	18 B2
Halcyon Cres. NR32	17 F4
Hall Dri. NR32	15 C4
Hall La, Blundeston. NR32	12 B2
Hall La, Oulton. NR32	16 B1
Hall Rd, Blundeston. NR32	12 A4
Hall Rd, Carlton Colville. NR33	18 A5
Hall Rd, Oulton. NR32	16 A4
Hamilton Rd. NR32	14 D4
Harbour Rd. NR32	16 C5
Hardy Clo. NR33	16 D6
Harebell Way. NR33	18 B2
Harold Rd. NR33	19 G2
Harps Close Rd. NR32	17 E3
Harrington Av. NR32	13 G6
Harris Av. NR32	17 F1
Harrison Rd. NR32	16 B5
Harrison Rd, Pakefield. NR33	19 F5
Harrop Dale. NR33	18 D5
*Harry Chamberlain Ct, Hopelyn Clo. NR32	17 E1
Harvest Dri. NR33	19 E5
Haven Av. NR32	17 E2
Haven Dale. NR33	18 C4
Haward St. NR32	14 A4
Hawthorn Av. NR33	19 E1
Healey Clo. NR32	13 E6
Heath La. NR32	12 A1
Heath Rd. NR33	16 D6
Heather Rd. NR32	17 G1
Hedley La. NR33	18 A4
Heigham Dri. NR33	19 E2
Henham Rd. NR32	17 E1
Herivan Gdns. NR32	16 B2
Herons Clo. NR32	15 D4
Herring Fishery Score. NR32	14 D3
Hervey St. NR32	14 A5
High Beech. NR32	17 E3
High St. NR32	14 C1
Higher Dri. NR32	16 C2
Highgrove Clo. NR32	16 D3
Highland Way. NR33	18 D1
Hildesley Ct. NR33	19 F4
Hill House Gdns. NR33	19 G2
Hill Rd. NR32	17 F4
Hillcrest Dri. NR32	17 E2
Hillcrest Gdns. NR32	17 E2
Hilltop Grn. NR32	17 E2
Hobart Clo. NR32	16 B2
Hobart Way. NR32	16 B2
Hogarth Walk. NR32	13 F6
Holbein Way. NR32	13 F5
Holbrook Rd. NR32	16 C2
Holden Clo. NR32	15 C4
Hollingsworth Rd. NR32	17 F2
Hollow Grove Way. NR33	18 B3
Hollow La. NR33	18 B3
Hollowell Clo. NR32	16 B2
Holly Rd. NR32	16 B5
Hollydene Clo. NR32	15 C3
Holme Ct. NR32	15 C3
Holst Clo. NR33	19 F2
Holton Av. NR32	16 C2
Homefield Av. NR33	19 E2
Honeysuckle Clo. NR33	19 E5
Hopelyn Clo. NR32	17 E1
Horn Hill. NR33	17 F6
Houghton Dri. NR32	16 B1
Howley Gdns. NR32	13 E5
Hubbards Av. NR32	13 G5
Hubbards Loke. NR32	13 G5
Huntingdon Clo. NR33	19 F5
INDUSTRIAL & RETAIL:	
Beach Ind Est. NR32	17 H3
Oulton Ind Est. NR32	16 B2
South Lowestoft Ind Est. NR33	19 E6
Ipswich Rd. NR32	14 B1
Irex Rd. NR33	19 F4
Ivy La. NR33	18 B1
Jacobs Ct. NR32	14 B3
Jacobs St. NR32	14 B3
Jasmine Grn. NR32	17 F3
Jeannie Mann Ct. NR32	17 E2
Jellicoe Av. NR33	18 C2
Jenkins Grn. NR32	13 E6
John Lang Ct. NR33	16 B6
John St. NR33	19 G1
Johnson Way. NR32	13 E6
Jubilee Rd. NR33	19 F6
Jubilee Way. NR32	14 C2
June Av. NR32	17 E3
Katwijk Way. NR32	14 B4
Keel Clo. NR33	18 A4
Kelly Pain Ct. NR32	17 F2
Kelsale Clo. NR32	16 D2
Kempshorne Clo. NR32	16 B1
Kendal Rd. NR33	19 G3
Kensington Rd. NR33	19 G2
Kent Rd. NR32	17 E4
Kesgrave Dri. NR32	16 C3
Kestral Grn. NR33	18 B2
Kevington Dri. NR32	15 C4
Kilbourn Rd. NR33	19 E5
Kimberley Rd. NR33	16 D6
Kingfisher Ct. NR33	18 B2
Kingston Clo. NR33	19 F4
Kingswood Av. NR33	18 C3
Kirby Cane Wk. NR32	16 D3
Kirkdale Ct. NR33	19 G4
Kirkley Cliff. NR33	19 H1
Kirkley Cliff Rd. NR33	19 G2
Kirkley Gdns. NR33	19 F2
Kirkley Park Rd. NR33	19 G2
Kirkley Run. NR33	19 F1
Kirkley St. NR33	19 G1
Kirkstone Way. NR32	16 D1
Kirkwood Dri. NR33	18 B4
Kittiwake Clo. NR33	18 C2
Knights Wood. NR32	13 F6
Lake View Rd. NR33	16 C6
Lakeland Dri. NR32	16 C4
Lakeside Rise. NR32	12 A4
Landspring La. NR33	18 D2
Langdale Pk. NR32	16 D1
Langley Gdns. NR33	19 E2
Lansdowne Rd. NR33	19 E4
Larch Rd. NR32	17 E3
Larkspur Clo. NR32	13 F4
Lattens Sq. NR32	14 A3
Laurel Rd. NR33	19 G2
Lavenham Way. NR32	16 D3
Lawrence Dri. NR32	13 F5
Lawson Rd. NR33	19 H1
Laxfield Way. NR33	19 E4
Leas Drift. NR33	18 B2
Leathes Clo. NR32	16 C4
Leiston Rd. NR32	14 C3
Leisure Way. NR32	13 E5
Leona Cres. NR33	18 B5
Leonard Dri. NR32	13 E5
Lighthouse Score. NR32	17 H2
Lilac Dri. NR32	17 E3
Lily Way. NR33	18 B3
Lime Av. NR32	15 D3
Lime Clo. NR32	15 D3
Links Clo. NR33	19 E3
Links Rd. NR32	13 H6
London Rd. NR33	19 F5
London Rd Nth. NR32	14 C5
London Rd Sth. NR33	19 F4
Long Acre. NR33	19 G4
Long Fields Path. NR32	16 B2
Long Meadow Wk. NR33	18 C3
Long Rd. NR33	18 D4
Longbeach Dri. NR33	18 C5
Longden Av. NR32	16 C4
Longfield Way. NR32	15 D3
Lorne Park Rd. NR33	19 G1
Lorne Rd. NR33	19 G1
Lothing St. NR32	16 C5
Lound Rd. NR32	12 A1
Love La. NR33	19 E4
Love Rd. NR32	14 A3
Lovewell Rd. NR33	19 G1
Low Farm Dri. NR33	18 B5
Lowestoft Rd. NR32	12 B3
Lowestoft Rd. NR33	18 C4
Lowry Way. NR32	13 G6
Loxley Rd. NR33	18 D1
Lucerne Clo. NR33	18 B3
Lulworth Pk. NR32	16 D2
Lymm Rd. NR32	17 E1
Lyncroft Rd. NR33	19 G4
Lyndhurst Rd. NR32	17 G2
Lyngate Av. NR33	18 D3
Lynton Gdns. NR32	17 F2
Magdalen Clo. NR32	16 D2
Magnolia Ct. NR32	17 E3
Maidstone Rd. NR32	14 A5
Mallow Way. NR33	18 B3
Maltsters Score. NR32	14 D3
Maltsters Way. NR32	16 A5
Malvern Rise. NR32	17 E2
Manor Ct. NR32	14 C2
Manor Park Rd. NR32	13 F2
Mantis Cres. NR32	17 E1
Maple Clo. NR32	12 D6
Maple Rd. NR33	19 E1
Marbella Grn. NR33	18 C3
Marham Rd. NR32	17 F3
Marina. NR32	14 C5
Marine Par. NR33	17 G6
Mariners Score. NR32	14 C2
Market La. NR32	12 B2
Marlborough Ct. NR32	16 C4
Marlborough Rd. NR32	16 C4
Marsden Clo. NR33	19 E5
Marsh La. NR33	18 A3
Marsh Rd. NR33	16 B6
Marshalls Piece. NR33	18 B2
Mast Clo. NR33	18 A4
Martello Rd. NR32	17 E1
Martin Clo. NR33	18 C5
Martins Av. NR33	19 G1
Martins Score. NR32	14 D2
Matlowck Dale. NR33	18 D5
Mautby Way. NR33	19 E3
May Rd. NR32	14 A4
Mayfield Rd. NR33	18 B4
Meadow Rd. NR32	16 C1
Meadow Way. NR33	18 B5
Meadowlands. NR32	12 B1
Meadowsweet Clo. NR33	18 C3
Melbourne Rd. NR32	14 B1
Melrose Clo. NR32	16 C1
Mendip Rd. NR32	16 B3
Merrifield Rd. NR33	19 E4
Merville. NR33	18 D5
Mews Ct. NR32	16 D1
Middle Way. NR32	13 G6
Mill Bank. NR32	16 C3
Mill La. NR32	13 G2
Mill Rd. NR33	17 F6
Miller Clo. NR33	19 F2
Mills Dri. NR32	13 G3
Milnes Way. NR33	18 A4
Milton Rd East. NR32	14 C3
Milton Rd West. NR32	14 B3
Mimosa Wk. NR32	17 E3
Minden Rd. NR32	14 A3
Minos Rd. NR32	17 F1
Mobbs Way. NR32	16 B3
Monarch Way. NR33	18 A5
Monckton Av. NR32	16 D3
Monckton Cres. NR32	16 D4
Monet Sq. NR32	13 F6
Monkshood Clo. NR33	19 E5
Montgomery Av. NR32	17 E2
Morton Rd. NR33	19 G3
Mount Pleasant. NR32	17 F2
Mountbatten Rd. NR32	17 E1
Moyes Rd. NR32	15 D4
Munnings Clo. NR33	18 B4
Murillo Dri. NR32	13 G6
Mutford Clo. NR32	16 C4
Mutfordwood La. NR33	18 A5
Mylodon Rd. NR32	17 F1
Myrtle Clo. NR32	17 E3
Nelson Rd. NR33	19 F4
Nelson Way. NR33	16 C6
Neptune St. NR32	17 F5
Newark Rd. NR33	19 G1
Newcombe Ct. NR32	16 A3
Newcombe Rd. NR32	14 D4
Newlands Clo. NR33	19 E4
Newsons Mdw. NR32	17 F3
Nicholson Sq. NR32	14 A3
Nidderdale. NR33	18 D5
Nightingale Rd. NR33	19 G4
Ninfield Clo. NR33	18 C4
Noel Rd. NR32	15 C4
Norfolk St. NR32	17 E4
Normandy Rd. NR32	17 E1
Normanshurst Clo. NR32	16 D3
Normanston Dri. NR32	16 C4
North Denes Sea Wall. NR32	17 H2
North Par. NR32	17 G2
Northfield Clo. NR32	12 D6
Northgate. NR32	17 E3
Northwood Clo. NR33	19 E2
Norwich Rd. NR32	14 A4
Notley Rd. NR33	19 F1
Oakwood Rd. NR33	19 E2
Oatlands Clo. NR33	18 C3
Ohio Clo. NR33	18 D4
Old Farm Rd. NR33	18 C3
Old La. NR32	13 F4
Old Market Sq. NR32	14 C3
Old Nelson St. NR32	14 C4
Olive Ct. NR32	17 E3
Oliver Clo. NR33	18 C5
Ontario Rd. NR33	19 G1
Orchard Av. NR33	18 D1
Orchard Clo. NR32	12 B1
Orchard Croft. NR33	18 C3

Orchard La. NR32 12 B2
Orford Dri. NR32 16 C2
Orwell Dri. NR32 16 D2
Osborne St. NR32 14 C1
Osprey Grn. NR33 18 C2
Oulton Ct. NR32 16 B2
Oulton Rd, Blundeston. NR32 12 D3
Oulton Rd, Lowestoft. NR32 17 E3
Oulton St. NR32 16 C1
Oxford Rd. NR32 14 B1

Paddock Hill. NR33 18 D1
Paddock Wood Clo. NR33 18 B4
Pakefield. NR33 19 F4
Pakefield Rd. NR33 19 G2
Pakefield St. NR33 19 G4
Palmer Clo. NR32 13 F5
Parade Rd Nth. NR3 14 B6
Parade Rd Sth. NR33 17 G6
Park Clo. NR33 18 C3
Park Rd. NR32 14 C2
Parkhill. NR32 12 D6
Parkholme Ter. NR32 17 G2
Parkside Dri. NR32 16 D4
Patricia Clo. NR32 15 D4
Patterdale Gdns. NR32 16 D1
Payne St. NR33 19 G1
Peacock Clo. NR33 18 B5
Peak Dale. NR33 18 D5
Pebble Clo. NR32 16 D2
Peddars Way. NR32 17 E2
Pegasus Mws. NR32 16 B5
Pembroke Way. NR32 16 D2
Pennine Way. NR32 16 C3
Penny La. NR32 16 C3
Pennygate Dri. NR33 18 D2
Pentland Wk. NR32 16 D2
Periwinkle Clo. NR33 18 B3
Peto Way. NR32 16 D1
Pier Ter. NR33 17 G6
Pinbush Clo. NR33 18 D5
Pinbush Rd. NR33 19 E5
Pinewood Av. NR33 19 E2
Planters Gro. NR33 19 E1
Pleasurewood Hill. NR32 13 E4
Plovers Way. NR33 18 C2
Plumtrees. NR32 15 C4
Police Station Rd. NR32 14 C4
Pollard Piece. NR33 18 B2
Poplar Rd. NR33 18 C4
Porthole Clo. NR33 18 A4
Portsch Clo. NR33 18 D4
Pound Farm Dri. NR32 16 C2
Pound La. NR32 12 B3
Primrose Clo. NR33 19 E5
Princes Rd. NR32 14 A2
Princes Wk. NR32 16 D4
Priors Clo. NR32 13 F6
Privet Grn. NR33 19 E1
Prospect Pl. NR33 19 G4
Prospect Rd. NR32 15 B5

Queens Highway. NR32 15 B4
Queens Rd. NR32 14 C1
Quinnell Way. NR32 13 E5

Raglan Rd. NR32 14 B3
Raglan St. NR32 14 B2
Rant Score. NR32 14 D3
Ranville. NR33 18 D5
Ranworth Av. NR33 18 D2
Raphael Walk. NR32 13 F6
Rectory Rd, Carlton Colville. NR33 18 B5
Rectory Rd, Lowestoft. NR33 19 G2
Red House Clo. NR32 16 C1
Redisham Clo. NR32 13 E6
Reeve St. NR32 14 B2
Regan Clo. NR32 13 E6
Regent Rd. NR32 14 C4
Rembrandt Clo. NR32 13 G6
Renoir Pl. NR32 13 F6
Reydon Mews. NR32 13 E6
Reynolds Walk. NR32 13 F6
Ribblesdale. NR33 18 D4
Richmond Rd. NR33 19 H1
Ridgeville. NR33 19 E5
Ringsfield Rd. NR32 16 D3
Rio Clo. NR33 18 B2
Rishton Rd. NR32 14 B4
Rivendale. NR33 18 C5
Riverside Rd. NR33 17 E6
Robertsbridge Way. NR33 18 C4
Robin Hill. NR32 17 E4
Rochdale. NR33 19 E5
Rochester Rd. NR33 19 G3
Rock Rd. NR32 15 D4
Rodber Way. NR32 13 E6
Roman Rd. NR32 14 A4
Romany Rd. NR32 15 C5
Romney Pl. NR32 13 F6
Rookery Clo. NR33 16 C6
Roosevelt Wk. NR33 18 B2
Rope Walk. NR33 18 B4
Rose Ct. NR32 17 E3
Rosedale Clo. NR33 18 D4
Rosedale Gdns. NR33 18 D4
Rosewood. NR33 19 E2
Rotterdam Rd. NR32 17 F3
Rounces La. NR33 18 B4
Rowan Way. NR33 18 C2
Rowntree Way. NR32 13 E6
Royal Av. NR32 17 G2
Royal Ter. NR33 17 G6
Roydon Way. NR32 16 C1
Rozlyne Clo. NR33 18 D4
*Rubens Walk, Sutherland Dri. NR32 13 F6
Ruby Clo. NR32 13 G3
Rumburgh Rd. NR32 17 E1
Run Mdw. NR33 18 B2
Rushlake Way. NR33 18 C4
Rushmere Rd. NR33 18 B6
Rye Clo. NR33 18 C3
Ryedale. NR33 18 D4

Saffron Sq. NR33 19 E5
St Catherines Clo. NR33 18 D3
St Georges Rd. NR33 19 G3
St Johns Rd. NR33 17 F6
St Leonards Rd. NR33 19 G1
St Margarets Plain. NR32 14 C2
St Margarets Rd. NR32 14 A1
St Michaels Clo. NR32 15 C4
*St Peters Ct, St Peters St. NR32 14 C2
St Peters Rd, Carlton Colville. NR33 18 B4
St Peters Rd, Lowestoft. NR33 19 G2
St Peters St. NR32 14 C2
St Quintons Ct. NR33 19 F3
Salisbury St. NR33 19 G1
Saltwater Way. NR33 16 B5
San Francisco Wk. NR33 18 B2
Sanctuary Gdns. NR32 16 C1
Sandbank Rd. NR33 18 D3
Sanders Clo. NR32 16 C2
Sandringham Rd. NR32 17 F4
Sands La. NR32 16 A3
Saturn Clo. NR32 17 G1
Saxon Rd. NR33 19 F4
School Rd. NR33 16 C6
Scroby Ct. NR32 15 C3
Seago St. NR32 14 B4
Seavert Clo. NR33 18 D4
Sedlescombe Rd. NR33 18 C3
Selby St. NR32 17 F5
Seven Acres. NR33 19 F5
Shadingfield Clo. NR32 13 E6
Sharon Dri. NR32 17 E2
Shaw Av. NR33 18 C5
Shelton Rd. NR33 19 E5
Ship Rd. NR33 19 E4
Shoals Wk. NR33 18 D2
Short La. NR33 18 B5
Short Rd. NR32 12 B2
Short St. NR33 19 G3
Silverwood Clo. NR33 19 F4
Siskin Grn. NR33 18 C2
Skamacre Cres. NR32 17 E4
Skoulding Clo. NR33 16 C6
Smiths Wk. NR33 18 B1
Snape Dri. NR32 16 D2
Somerleyton Rd, Lowestoft. NR32 16 C1
Somerleyton Rd, Somerleyton. NR32 12 A3
Somerton Av. NR32 14 A1
Sotterley Clo. NR32 13 E6
Sotterley Rd. NR32 16 D2
South Elmham Ter. NR33 16 B6
South Leet Clo. NR31 16 B2
South View Clo. NR32 17 E4
Southfield Gdns. NR33 19 E2
Southwell Rd. NR33 19 G1
Spashett Rd. NR32 17 E1
Speedwell Clo. NR33 19 E5
Spencer Dri. NR32 13 F6
Spexall Way. NR32 17 E1
Springfield Gdns. NR33 19 E2
Spruce Ct. NR32 17 F3
Spurgeon Score. NR32 14 D3
Squires Walk. NR32 13 G6
Stafford Ct. NR32 16 C2
Stanford St. NR32 14 A4
Stanley Rd. NR33 16 C6
Stanley St. NR32 14 B4
Stansfield Clo. NR33 18 D1
Stanton Clo. NR32 14 G6
Staplehurst Clo. NR33 18 B4
Station Rd, Corton. NR32 13 G2
Station Rd, Lowestoft. NR32 17 G2
Station Sq. NR32 17 G5
Stayngate Wk. NR32 16 B2
Stephensons Wk. NR32 17 G1
Stevens St. NR32 17 F5
Stimpson Clo. NR32 13 E5
Stirling Clo. NR32 16 C1
Stirrups La. NR32 12 D1
Stoven Clo. NR32 17 E1
Stradbroke Rd. NR33 19 E4
Stubbs Wood. NR32 13 F5
Suffolk Rd. NR32 14 C5
Summer Rd. NR32 14 B4
Summerfield Gdns. NR33 19 E2
Sunningdale Av. NR33 19 G4
Sunny Fields. NR33 16 D6
Surrey St. NR32 14 B5
Sussex Rd. NR32 17 G2
Sutherland Dri. NR32 13 F5
Swallowfields. NR33 18 C5
Swift Clo. NR33 18 C4
Swonnells Wk. NR32 16 A5
Sycamore Av. NR33 18 C1

Tansy Clo. NR33 19 E5
Tedder Rd. NR32 17 E2
Teesdale. NR33 18 D5
Telesia Ct. NR32 17 E1
Tennyson Rd. NR32 14 C3
Tenterden Clo. NR33 18 C3
The Avenue. NR33 19 F2
The Boulevard. NR33 16 B5
The Brindles. NR33 18 D4
The Close. NR32 13 G2
The Cut. NR32 13 G2
The Drive. NR32 16 C3
The Eddies. NR33 18 D3
The Fairway. NR33 18 D3
The Firs. NR33 18 B5
The Gap. NR33 19 E1
The Gardens. NR33 18 B6
The Glades. NR32 15 D4
The Green. NR33 19 E1
The Greylings. NR33 18 C4
The Hemplands. NR32 14 C1
The Homestead. NR33 18 C4
The Leas. NR32 12 D6
The Loke. NR32 12 B1
The Meads. NR32 17 F1
The Parklands. NR33 18 C3
The Pastures. NR32 12 D6
The Pippins. NR32 12 B1
The Prarie. NR32 14 C5
The Ravine. NR32 17 G2
The Ridgeways. NR33 18 C3
The Shires. NR32 13 F4
The Sound. NR33 18 D3
The Staithe. NR33 18 D2
The Street, Blundeston. NR32 12 B1
The Street, Corton. NR32 13 G2
The Street, Oulton. NR33 18 B5
The Trossachs. NR32 15 D3
The Venlaw. NR33 19 G2
The Weald. NR32 16 B3
The Woodlands. NR32 13 F4
Thirlmere Wk. NR32 16 D2
Thistledown. NR33 18 C3
Thornham Clo. NR33 19 E4
Thornycroft Gdns. NR33 18 A5
Thurne Rd. NR33 19 E2
Thurston Rd. NR32 14 C2
Till Rd. NR32 14 B4
Tonning St. NR32 14 A5
Tower Rd. NR33 19 E6
Townsend Way. NR32 13 E6
Trafalgar St. NR32 14 A5
Tramps Alley. NR32 13 H4
*Triangle Yd, St Peters St. NR32 14 C3
Trinity Rd. NR32 14 D4
Tudor Wk. NR33 18 D4
Tunstall Dri. NR32 16 C2
Turnberry Clo. NR33 19 E3
Turner Clo. NR32 13 F6

Ubbeston Way. NR33 19 E4
Uggleshall Clo. NR32 16 D1
Ullswater. NR33 18 C5
Underwood Clo. NR 12 D6
Union La. NR32 16 C1
Union Pl. NR33 19 H1
Union Rd. NR32 14 A4
Uplands Clo. NR33 18 C3
Uplands Rd Sth. NR33 18 B4
Uplands Rd Nth. NR33 18 C3
Upper Esplanade. NR33 19 H2

Vallibus Clo. NR32 16 B2
Van Dyke Clo. NR32 13 F6
Velda Clo. NR33 18 D4
Verdure Clo. NR32 12 D6
Vermeer Clo. NR32 13 F5
Viburnum Grn. NR32 17 F3
Victoria Rd. NR33 16 B6
Village Way. NR32 13 F6

Wainwright Clo. NR32 13 E5
Walberswick Way. NR32 16 D3
Walcott Wk. NR33 19 F3
Walmer Rd. NR33 19 F2
Walton Rd. NR32 14 A4
Wannock Clo. NR33 18 C4
Warren La. NR32 12 A5
Warren Rd. NR32 17 G1
Water La. NR32 14 A1
Waters Av. NR33 18 B5
Waveney Cres. NR33 17 C6
Waveney Dri. NR33 16 D6
Waveney Hill. NR32 15 B5
Waveney Rd. NR32 14 C5
Wayne Clo. NR32 13 F6
Wedgewood Ct. NR32 17 G2
Wellington Esp. NR33 19 H1
Wellington Rd. NR33 19 F4
Wenhaston Way. NR32 16 C2
Wensleydale. NR33 18 D4
Wentworth Way. NR33 19 E3
Wesley St. NR32 14 B2
West Gro. NR33 19 F4
West Side Clo. NR32 13 F6
Westhall Rd. NR32 16 D1
Westland Rd. NR33 18 D1
Weston Rd. NR32 17 E1
Westwood Av. NR33 18 D2
Whapload Rd. NR32 14 D4
Wharfdale. NR33 18 D4
Wheatacre Dri. NR32 13 F2
Wheatfield Rd. NR33 18 C3
*Whinland Wk, Breckland Way. NR32 16 D2
Whiskin Clo. NR32 15 D4
White Horse St. NR32 14 C2
Whiting Rd. NR32 15 C3
Whitton Clo. NR33 18 D1
Whitton Ct. NR33 19 E1
Wiggs Way. NR32 13 G2
Wildes Score. NR32 14 D4
Wildes St. NR32 14 D3
Willow Rd. NR33 19 F5
Willowbrook Clo. NR33 18 A4
Willowvale Clo. NR32 12 D6
Wilson Rd. NR33 19 G3
Windermere Pk. NR32 16 D1
Windsor Rd. NR33 17 F6
Windward Way. NR33 18 D2
Winnipeg Rd. NR32 14 B1
Winston Av. NR33 18 D1
Wissett Way. NR32 17 E1
Witney Green. NR33 19 F4
Witney Rd. NR33 19 F4
Wollaston Rd. NR32 14 B4
Wood La. NR32 15 C2
Woodlands Av. NR33 18 B5
Woodpecker Av. NR33 18 C2
Woods Loke E. NR32 16 D3
Woods Loke W. NR32 16 C3
Woodside Clo. NR33 18 B4
Worlingham Way. NR32 16 D2
Worthing Rd. NR32 17 G2

Yarmouth Rd, Corton. NR32 12 D2
Yarmouth Rd, Lowestoft. NR32 17 F1
Yarrow Dri. NR33 18 B3
Yeovil Rd. NR32 14 A3
Yew Dale. NR33 18 C5
York Rd. NR32 17 F4

Edition 541-04 08.03